WINNER! WINNER!
CHICKEN
DINNER

WINNER! WINNER! CHICKEN DINNER

50 Winning Ways to Cook It Up!

Stacie Billis

Storey Publishing

The mission of Storey Publishing is to serve our customers by
publishing practical information that encourages
personal independence in harmony with the environment.

Edited by Deanna F. Cook and Lisa H. Hiley
Art direction and book design by Ash Austin
Text production by Liseann Karandisecky
Indexed by Andrea Chesman

Cover photography by © Dominic Perri,
     except back cover, author photo by Leah Flores
Interior photography by © Dominic Perri
Additional photography by © Fertnig/
     iStock.com, 17; © xxmmxx/iStock.com
     18 (wood cutting board); © praphab144/
     stock.adobe.com, 24; © Foodcollection RF/
     Getty Images, 49; © phive2015/iStock.com, 51;
     © yevtony/iStock.com, 58; © Irina Rostokina/
     Shutterstock.com, 127
Photo styling by Ann Lewis
Food styling by Joy Howard
Graphics by Ash Austin

Text © 2020 by Stacie Billis

Storey books are available at special discounts
when purchased in bulk for premiums and
sales promotions as well as for fund-raising
or educational use. Special editions or book
excerpts can also be created to specification.
For details, please call 800-827-8673, or send
an email to sales@storey.com.

Storey Publishing
210 MASS MoCA Way
North Adams, MA 01247
storey.com

Printed in China through Asia Pacific Offset
10 9 8 7 6 5 4 3 2

Library of Congress Cataloging-in-Publication Data

Names: Billis, Stacie, author.
Title: Winner! winner! chicken dinner : 50 winning
     ways to cook it up! / Stacie Billis.
Description: North Adams : Storey Publishing, 2020.
     | Includes index. | Summary: "Home cooks
     can prepare delicious chicken suppers with
     confidence and ease. Each chapter is chock-
     full of tips and tricks that use a wide range
     of techniques, from braising and roasting to
     grilling, slow cooking, and sheet-pan cooking"—
     Provided by publisher.
Identifiers: LCCN 2019051396 (print) | LCCN
     2019051397 (ebook) | ISBN 9781635861563
     (paperback) | ISBN 9781635861570 (ebook)
Subjects: LCSH: Cooking (Chicken) | LCGFT:
     Cookbooks.
Classification: LCC TX750.5.C45 B5 2020
     (print) | LCC TX750.5.C45 (ebook) | DDC
     641.6/65—dc23
LC record available at https://lccn.loc.
     gov/2019051396
LC ebook record available at https://lccn.loc.
     gov/2019051397

TO ISAAC AND OLIVER
Thank you for sharing me with my work,
even when it means eating
mostly chicken for a year.
(Hey, at least it's delicious chicken!)

Also, to all the busy home cooks working
overtime to make cooking fit your life:
Thank you for trusting me, and keep going.
You're doing even better than you know.

CONTENTS

PREFACE

How can I be so sure chicken is what's on your table? Because according to the USDA, for the first time in 100 years, chicken is more popular than beef in the United States. In the 1950s, Americans ate an average of 16 pounds of chicken per person every year. By 2000, that number had grown to a whopping 53 pounds per year. It's easy to understand why when you think about how versatile, family-friendly, quick-cooking, budget-friendly, and lean chicken can be.

You know what else chicken can be? Boring, bland, and easily overcooked.

In fact, for a long time, in the fine dining world, the chicken dish was the throwaway on the menu. It was the option for the customer with the uncultivated palate. But it certainly doesn't have to be. And anyone who's had perfectly cooked chicken — maybe your grand-mother's succulent roasted bird, your neighbor's famous fried chicken, the mouthwatering wings you can't stop thinking about from your travels, or the chicken slathered in a pungent garlic sauce at your local Lebanese shawarma joint — knows this to be true.

Chicken can be ethereally delicious stuffed with the fanciest ingredients at a Michelin-starred restaurant in New York City or simply grilled the way you might grab a skewer beachside in Mexico.

Or just cooked at home using the right recipe that I hope you'll find using this cookbook.

One could easily write a tome on chicken. Every culture eats it. There are thousands upon thousands of chicken recipes, and hundreds that count as classics. You can cook chicken using nearly every home cooking technique and, considering that most birds weigh in around three and a half to four pounds, the number of ways that you can get the meat — in any combination of boneless, skinless, thin or thick cut, broken into individual pieces, joint pieces, whole, or ground — is amazing.

But this isn't that comprehensive cookbook.

Instead, this is a vibrant, fun, easy, and ultimately, practical collection of chicken recipes that can help busy cooks — you! — solve dinnertime and even have some fun. Like maybe have friends over and impress them? And if they have kids, have their kids hap-pily eat dinner, too?

How's that for impressive *and* practical?

My hope is that this will become your favorite kitchen handbook — all splattered and dog-eared — that shares the fundamentals and houses a fantastic collec-tion of go-to recipes. Given how much chicken you're cooking, I hope that this book inspires and empowers you to riff on your own chicken dishes as well.

MOVE OVER, BEEF.

CHICKEN IS WHAT'S FOR DINNER.

Stacie Billis

PART 1
CHOOSING, BUYING & HANDLING

With chicken, as with most dishes, a great end result relies on good choices from the start. Choosing the right cut for your recipe; buying fresh meat from happy, healthy birds; and handling your chicken safely are the first steps to ensure that your chicken dinner will turn out a winner.

CHOOSING THE RIGHT CUT FOR YOUR DISH

IF YOU ASK ME, there are no hard-and-fast rules for home cooks: you should cook what you like. Fortunately, chicken is forgiving. You'll get the hang of which cuts work best for which types of recipes by cooking through this book. But some rules of thumb will help you understand decisions I've made for recipes and also guide you as you begin cooking your own chicken dishes.

GO WHOLE HOG, OR MAKE THAT WHOLE CHICKEN. Whenever possible, cut up a whole chicken rather than buy precut pieces. If you're game, this will save you tons of money over the long haul. Whole chickens are less expensive than individual parts, especially if you're going for higher-quality meat. Which brings me to my second point: it's often easier to find higher-quality whole birds.

Once you break down the chicken, you'll have two breast pieces, two legs, two thighs, and two wings, plus some scraps. I usually save the scraps and wings in a food storage bag in the freezer; when enough has collected, I make homemade stock (which saves even more money!).

When choosing a whole bird — either to cut up or cook whole — go for one that's three and a half to four pounds. Anything larger will likely taste bland. If you need more meat, opt for a second bird.

You don't always need to use a whole bird when roasting, however. i happen to love roasting whole birds the classic way, but you can roast chicken pieces with the same method in less time. In fact, it's especially convenient to use pieces if your family has strong opinions about certain cuts. If everyone prefers white meat, for example, why roast a whole bird when you can serve them all skin-on, bone-in breasts instead?

CHICKEN BREASTS FOR SHOWCASING SAUCES. Boneless chicken breasts, the butt of rubber-chicken dinner jokes, serve an important purpose. Really, they do! The quick-cooking cut makes the perfect base for just about any flavor addition. Delicious dressings, dipping sauces, and pan gravies are the most underused secret weapons that busy cooks don't know they have (until now!). They can be made quickly, some even ahead of time, and take a simple dinner from plain to fantastic with just a handful of fresh, on-hand ingredients. Anytime you need a fast dinner that features a fragrant sauce — think a sauté, something cooked *en papillote*, or a stir-fry — chicken breasts are your go-to.

CHICKEN CUTLETS FOR A 15-MINUTE MEAL. Need dinner even faster? Thin-cut chicken breasts, a.k.a. chicken cutlets, are the way to go. And while you could dress them in a sauce, you could also simply dust them with spices or breadcrumbs. Whatever works with a quick flash in the pan.

THIGH MEAT FOR JUICY DELICIOUSNESS. Unless I'm in a rush, whenever a recipe calls for chicken breast, I consider swapping in boneless, skinless chicken thighs. They act much the same, but have tons more flavor thanks to a higher fat content. They are also easier to cook without drying out for the same reason.

BONE-IN, SKIN-ON PIECES FOR MAXIMUM FLAVOR. Whenever you want to build deep, rich flavor, start by browning chicken that still has skin on, even if you will eventually braise, slow cook, pressure-cook, or otherwise prepare the meat in a way that will soften the skin in the end. The flavor you build while browning the meat will elevate the overall flavor of your dish, and you can always remove soggy skin from the meat before serving.

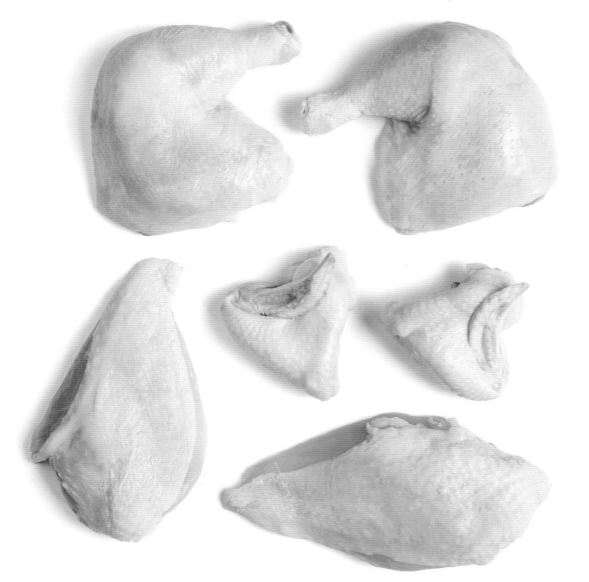

BUYING TASTY, HEALTHY CHICKEN

A DELICIOUS CHICKEN DISH starts with buying delicious chicken. Putting aside a conversation about values, taste tests — both my own and those conducted by food publications — confirm that premium chickens, including organic and free-range birds sold by smaller companies such as Bell & Evans, D'Artagnan, and Belle Rouge, tend to be tastier.

And though I can't vouch for what you'll find at your local butcher, chances are the chicken at an independent butcher will be supremely more delicious if the birds come from local farms.

If you're willing to spend extra money to get quality meat but aren't sure which brands are best, conduct some of your own taste tests. Keep in mind that a single brand may not be best across every cut.

Here are some features to look for when buying chicken.

CHILLED IN AIR, NOT WATER. Once chickens are killed, drained, and plucked, the USDA requires that the temperature of the carcasses be lowered to at least 40°F (4°C) within four hours of slaughter. To achieve this, they are chilled, typically en masse, in a water bath. During this step, the bird can retain as much as 14 percent water, and sometimes the water is chlorinated (safe, but good to know). This water retention should be noted on the label, and rightly so since it negatively impacts taste and texture. Plus, it increases the weight of the meat, which also impacts price.

Air-chilled birds are hung in the open while cold, purified air circulates, bringing the temperature of the meat down to the required minimum temperature in about three and a half hours. This process does not dry the chicken out or add any moisture or weight. It also reduces the risk of bacterial contamination.

ORGANIC. Whether or not you generally buy organic groceries, this is the most meaningful label when it comes to supermarket chicken. Regulated by the USDA, organic chicken comes from birds raised without antibiotics, fed organic feed made without animal by-products, and given access to the outdoors.

This last point is pretty important: the more a chicken moves, the better it will taste. However, the organic label does *not* regulate how much time the bird must spend outside. An organic bird raised on a large, industrial-type organic farm may not see very much outside time. This is often why chickens from local farms that actually run around outdoors taste more delicious.

ANTIBIOTIC-FREE. This can be a tricky label. If you're committed to antibiotic-free chicken, you'll want to look specifically for terms like *raised without antibiotics* or *no antibiotics ever.* Just keep in mind that enforcement is not strict except for when there is also an organic label, in which case you'll need to look for the USDA organic seal *and* the *raised without antibiotics* label.

Organic alone does not guarantee zero use of antibiotics since they can be administered in the hatchery while the chick is still in the egg.

Other labels, such as *hormone-free*, *natural*, *all-natural*, *vegetarian-fed*, *cage-free*, and *free-range*, have very little applied meaning. And while the labels *kosher* and *halal* mean something specific about how chickens are processed, they don't necessarily signify anything about the quality, taste, or texture of the chicken. You'll have to include individual brands in your taste test to see how they measure up.

BRINGING CHICKEN TO ROOM TEMPERATURE

Food safety is, of course, of paramount importance. When I suggest that you allow chicken (whole or parts) to sit on the counter for up to an hour before cooking, the purpose is to bring the meat up to room temperature. It does not mean — nor am I advocating — that chicken sit at the warm temperatures that foster food-borne pathogens for an extended period of time. Provided you're working with quality meat, allowing it to sit on the counter for up to an hour in order to come to room temperature (not warmer) before cooking should not cause a problem. This is just my recommendation, not a requirement for success.

The reason for doing this is that it helps for more even cooking, which also makes for juicier meat. Think about it this way: if the temperature of the meat is higher to begin with, it will cook faster. This evens out the cooking time of the inner meat with the meat closer to the surface and also cuts down cooking time slightly overall, reducing the chance of overcooking.

That's why you'll always see notes at the end of a recipe about checking the temperature and allowing for more cook time if needed. The range of cooking time covers variability in the size of the piece of meat, the cook's technique, oven/stove variability, and the temperature the meat was to begin with going into cooking.

SAFE HANDLING

ONCE YOU CHOOSE YOUR CUT and make your purchase, it's all about safe handling. Even fresh-from-the-farm birds can contain dangerous bacteria. Following a few simple rules keeps the meat from developing into a health hazard on its way from kitchen counter to dining room table.

ALWAYS KEEP YOUR CHICKEN REFRIGERATED. Put raw chicken away as soon as you get home from the market, and pack leftovers in a sealed container to store in the fridge as soon as they have cooled to room temperature.

DON'T WASH CHICKEN. It's not necessary and can actually spread harmful bacteria.

KEEP RAW CHICKEN AWAY FROM OTHER FOOD. Before you start prepping chicken, clear your work area to prevent cross contamination with other ingredients. This is especially important for ingredients that will be served raw, as in a salad.

WASH, WASH, WASH. Always wash hands, knives, counters, the sink, and anything else that comes in contact with raw meat, chicken juices, or your chicken-besmirched hands with soap and very hot water. See the next section about having a dedicated cutting board.

COOK TO THE PROPER TEMPERATURE. According to the USDA, chicken should be cooked to an internal temperature of at least 165°F (75°C). Some new guidelines say that chicken breasts can be more like 140 to 145°F (60–62°C) before resting and that thighs, bone-in pieces, and whole birds can be 155 to 160°F (68–70°C) before resting. I personally prefer these new temperatures to avoid drying out the chicken, but have given the USDA recommendations for safety.

Decide what feels right for you, but know that if you opt to cook your chicken to 165°F (75°C), you will still end up with juicy meat as long as you don't go over that temp. The key: invest in a meat thermometer! Otherwise, you'll always need to err on the side of safety and, when playing a guessing game, it's really easy to overcook chicken, with unfortunate results. Being able to cook chicken just up to that safe place, while keeping it juicy and tender, makes all the difference and is worth every dime you'll pay for a meat thermometer.

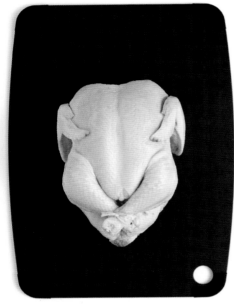

Have a Separate Cutting Board

Keep a dedicated cutting board for chicken (or for all meat and fish). You've no doubt heard this advice before, and I'm here to say that you should be following it. I'm all for keeping a simple kitchen, but with proper care, owning a dedicated chicken/meat/fish cutting board will greatly reduce the risk of harmful cross contamination.

The recommendation used to be that a cutting board for meat should be plastic. While a brand-new plastic cutting board can be very easy to disinfect, newer research shows that used plastic surfaces harbor as much bacteria as, if not more bacteria than, their weathered wooden counterparts. The best option is the hardest option, and in the long run, that's usually a cutting board made from the hardest wood you can find, like maple or beech. High-end cutting boards made from extremely hard plastics fabricated specifically to combat cross contamination are great, too.

Properly wash *and* dry your cutting board after handling chicken. Start by rinsing all the debris off the board. Be careful not to splatter the debris everywhere since you'll have to wash this area thoroughly, too. Then scrub your board with soap and hot water; plastic cutting boards can go in the dishwasher. Either way, once it's clean, dry the board thoroughly by hand before storing it, even if this just means wiping up a few drops of water that the dishwasher didn't dry. Bacteria need moisture to grow!

In addition to regular cleanings, deep clean and disinfect your dedicated meat cutting board monthly with a bleach solution made by combining a gallon of water with a tablespoon of bleach. Rinse thoroughly with water and dry completely.

Replace cutting boards once they become heavily knife-marked. Those cuts and crevices are where bacteria hide, even from your most valiant washing and disinfecting efforts.

CLEAN, CLEANER, CLEANEST

There is some debate about whether you should disinfect your cutting board and kitchen work area periodically or after *every time* you prep chicken. If you have strong concerns about food-borne illness and/or eat chicken very frequently, you should consider disinfecting frequently.

Also, you might consider increased vigilance if/when you opt for mass-market chicken given the prevalence of bacteria in the big conglomerates' chicken supply chain.

The bleach solution mentioned, which has a two-week shelf life, works well for cleaning everything, from boards to knives, sinks to counters. Because of the nature of how chemicals bind to wood, though, some suggest that wooden cutting boards are better disinfected using a solution made with quaternary ammonium. Look for it on the label of common spray cleaners like Fantastik and Mr. Clean, where you can also find directions for concocting a disinfecting solution with water. Clorox and Purell both make a quaternary ammonium surface cleaner.

TOOLS OF THE TRADE

As a reformed kitchen gadget junkie, I can attest to the long list of tools you could buy to be prepared for every cluckin' scenario possible, from a cleaver (for hacking away at chicken parts to make stock) to a splatter shield and skimmer (for deep-frying boneless, skinless thighs). But they aren't absolutely necessary.

The following tools, on the other hand, are. Or at least they are useful enough across all of your cooking tasks that you should have them in your kitchen anyway.

Dedicated Cutting Board

We went over this already: I strongly suggest that you keep a separate chicken or chicken/meat/fish cutting board. I prefer to use one made of hard wood, such as maple, but whatever the material, make sure to replace it when it is heavily knife-marked.

Boning Knife

If you plan to cut up your own whole chickens, which I strongly recommend (saves money, cuts down on waste, and makes it easier to get all the cuts you want from a healthy, happy bird), the sharp point and narrow blade of a 5- to 6-inch boning knife will make life much easier.

Chef's Knife

If you don't already own an 8- to 10-inch chef's knife, you'll want one for working with chicken. In particular, you'll need it to cut through the joints when breaking down a chicken and also for cutting boneless breast and thighs for curries, stir-fries, stews, and the like. You'll also want it for cutting cooked chicken, from carving a whole roasted bird to slicing cooked cutlets.

Paring Knife

This is another knife that you probably own — or should. For prepping chicken, you'll use it to trim fat, remove tendons, and cut tenders.

Kitchen Shears

I use my kitchen shears for everything, but when it comes to chicken, they're particularly great for cutting out the backbone when I want to butterfly my bird. If you have lightweight kitchen shears and want to use them for this purpose, you may want to consider upgrading or investing in heavy-duty poultry shears.

Instant-Read Thermometer

According to the USDA, it's imperative to cook chicken to an internal temperature of at least 165°F (75°C). The most reliable way to know that you've done so is with an instant-read thermometer. Without one, you're at high risk for over- or undercooking your chicken, which is bad news. (See pages 15–16.)

Fish Spatula

What's fish got to do with our fowl? I'm a huge fan of my fish spatula, which I use as an all-purpose spatula. Fish spatulas have a thin, flexible blade and beveled edge that allow them to slide easily underneath anything, including browned meat that may be sticking to the pan in spots.

If you've browned your meat properly, it shouldn't stick to the pan at all, but let's be real: it happens to the best of us. This tool will help keep your meat or that crispy skin from tearing, which means a lot to a busy home cook.

Roasting Pan and Rack

If you ask me, home cooks shouldn't worry too much about their roasting pan. Unless you're in the market for a new one or just beginning to equip your kitchen, whatever you have will work fine. Otherwise, look for a triple-ply roaster that comes with a basket rack or V-rack, which are more effective at allowing air to circulate while the bird cooks. This helps yield crispier skin all around.

Most great roasting pans come in larger sizes — 16 or 17 inches — which is nice for the occasional times when you'll need to cook a large turkey or two chickens at once. If that will never be necessary, you can look for a smaller roasting pan, or perhaps consider using a cast-iron skillet for your everyday roasting. (To be clear: you won't pair a rack with your cast-iron skillet.)

If you already have a roasting pan, but don't have a rack, don't freak out. This is solved in one of several easy ways. You can skip the rack and prop your bird on veggies instead. The skin in contact with the vegetables may not crisp, but at least it won't stick to the pan. You can also roast your bird in a preheated cast-iron skillet. When you place the bird on the hot surface, the dark meat on the bottom will start cooking, which builds flavor and helps with more even cooking.

And of course, you can buy a rack. Just make sure to get one that fits snugly in your roasting pan.

PART 2

BUTCHERING & CARVING

FOR THE EVERYDAY COOK

SORRY. I'M NOT GOING TO HELP YOU BECOME A BUTCHER. Butchering is an art perfected with training over time. This chapter is not meant to guide you through that level of coaching or practice.

Instead, I will walk you through how to break down a bird and do a few other things that are handy when cooking chicken frequently at home. I'll make sure that you know how to handle chicken safely and expertly enough to get delicious results as quickly and simply as possible, using fresh and easily accessible ingredients.

It may not sound quite as cool as being a butcher, but you'll thank me in the end. I promise.

BEFORE YOU START!

Aside from pulling out your dedicated cutting board, make sure that your knives are sharp. It may sound counterintuitive, but a dull knife is dangerous. That's not to say that you can't get in trouble with a sharp knife (you can!), but the duller the knife, the harder you have to press on it to cut, which is bad news if the knife slips and your finger is in the way.

HOW TO
Cut Up a Whole Chicken

The key to successfully breaking down a chicken is cutting through the joints (easy), not the bone (hard). Finding the joints is all about locating articulation. When you first start breaking down chickens, don't be afraid to move the joints with one hand while feeling around with the other — wiggle the wing, shake the drumstick, shimmy the thigh.

The goal is to find that place where the joints meet so that you can identify the space between them. That's where you want to cut.

I recommend using a 5- to 6-inch boning knife for everything except cutting through the joints and splitting the breast, which I find easier to do with an 8- to 10-inch chef's knife. I also like removing the backbone with heavy-duty kitchen shears.

That sounds like a lot of gear, I know. If you only have an 8- to 10-inch chef's knife, that's fine, too.

Let's get started . . .

If you're working with a mass-produced bird, start by checking the cavity for packed giblets and remove them.

1. Remove the wings.

Place the chicken on its side on your cutting board. Gently pull the wing away from the body. Without going too deep, stick the tip of your knife into the hollow where the wing meets the breast and cut around the joint, releasing the wing. Repeat with the other wing.

If you're going to cook the wings, use your chef's knife or kitchen shears to cut off the wing tip (keep for making stock), and then to cut through the joint connecting the remaining parts of the wing.

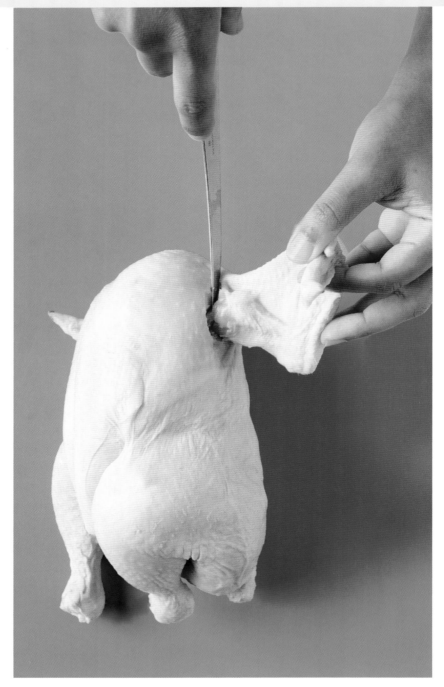

2. Remove the leg quarters,
which are the connected drumstick and thigh.

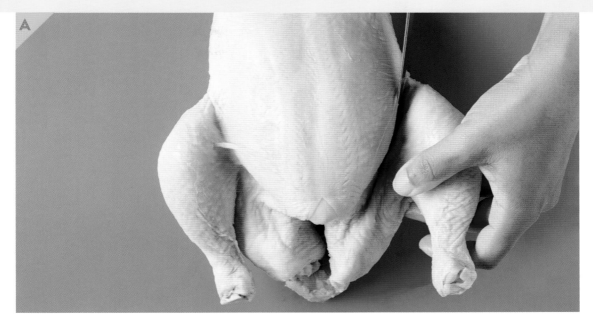

A | Make sure the chicken is breast side up. Gently pull a leg away from the body and use the tip of your knife to cut into the excess skin (just the skin!) between the leg and the body. Be careful not to cut very deeply.

B | Put the knife down, grab the leg with your dominant hand and stabilize the chicken with your other hand. In one swift, easy motion, twist the leg away from the body and down toward the cutting board to pop the drumstick joint out of its socket. This should happen pretty easily.

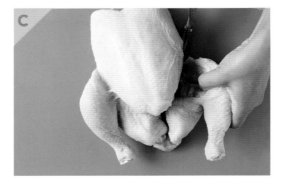

C | Now you can make your final cut to release the leg quarters: holding the leg away from the body, cut through the joint you just popped and the skin, too, in order to fully release it.

Repeat steps A, B, and C with the other leg.

3. If you want, split the leg quarters.

If you want separate drumsticks and thighs, split each leg quarter. To find the joint between the leg and thigh, flip each leg quarter over and look for the fat line between where the drumstick and thigh meet. That's exactly where you want to cut.

To double-check that you're in the right place, move the drumstick back and forth with one hand while your other feels around for the joint. Once you're sure that you've found it, cut straight down. Your knife should cut easily into the space between the joint. If you meet a lot of resistance, you're not in the right spot.

FOR BONELESS THIGHS

ONCE THE THIGH IS SEPARATED from the drumstick, you can debone it as well. Flip it skin side down and use your boning knife to cut along the length of one side of the bone, staying as close to it as possible and angling your knife to get slightly under it. Repeat this cut on the other side, after which you should be able to slide your knife completely under the bone to cut it free from underneath as well.

Once you've cut all the way around the bone, use your hands to pull it free. Just notice: if any meat begins to tear significantly, use your knife to cut the meat loose. After the bone has been removed, be sure to also remove any remaining hard pieces of cartilage and trim any extra fat.

4. Remove the backbone.

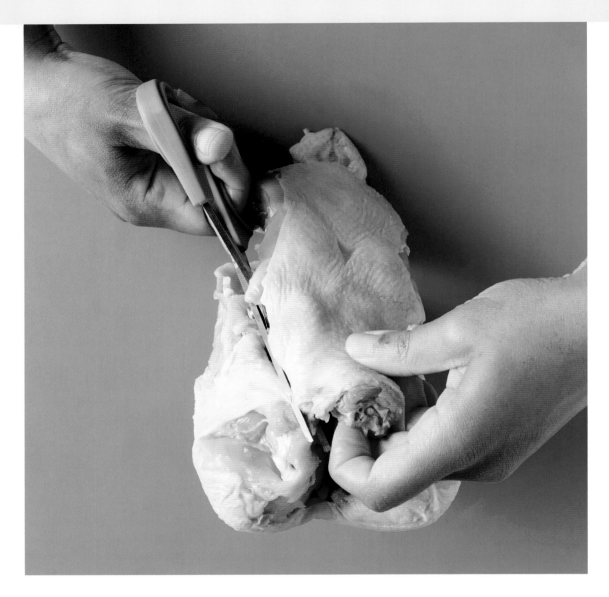

By now you're left with just the body of your bird. Prop up the chicken so it's resting on the neck flap, with the large cavity opening facing upward. You'll see a vertical line of fat on each side of the carcass between the rib cage and the breast: this is where you want to cut, either with a very sharp chef's knife or your kitchen shears. Follow the fat line all the way down, through the ribs. If it helps, you can use your hands to snap the backbone, then continue cutting.

Once you cut the backbone free, you'll be left with a whole breast.

5. Split the breast.

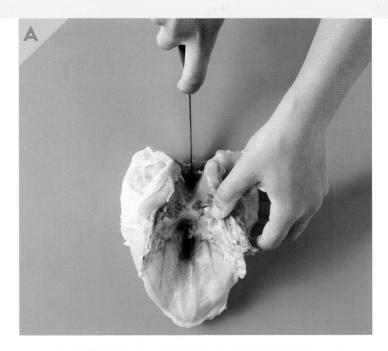

A | Flip the breast over so it is skin side down and find the wishbone, which is the only bone that you have to cut through in order to split the breast (the rest is cartilage). Crack it by pressing down hard with your knife.

B | Flip the breast over and, starting from the split wishbone, use your chef's knife to cut straight down the middle of the breast.

GOING SKINLESS: Once you break down a whole bird, you can make any of the pieces skinless by simply pulling the skin off with your fingers. Any "film" left on the chicken — technically called fat cap — is okay to eat. Tasty, even.

IF YOU WANT BONELESS BREASTS, you have to split the breast using a different method altogether. In step 5, keep the whole breast on your cutting board skin side up and carefully run your boning knife down one side of the white strip of cartilage that splits the whole breast, hugging the cartilage as tight as possible (A).

As you get toward the bottom, you'll hit the wishbone and rib cage. Just follow the curvature until the breast half is cut free; on the left side that will mean curving to the left and on the right side it will mean curving to the right (B). Repeat on the other side.

While this part sounds easy, it can be quite tricky given that the cartilage is soft and easy to cut through. It won't guide you the same way that bones will, but you'll get the hang of it after some practice.

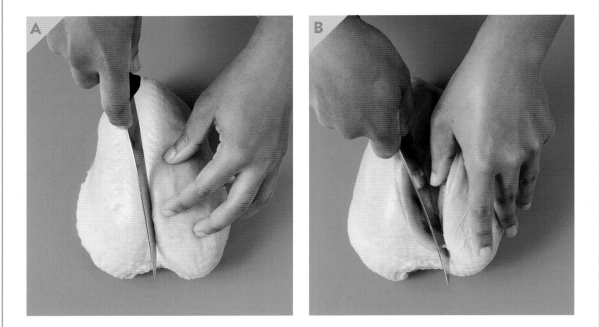

HOW TO
Butterfly a Whole Bird

This section was originally called How to Spatchcock a Whole Bird, because *spatchcock* is such a glorious word. But as it turns out, writing *spatchcock* many times over gets tiresome. So here we are with *butterfly*. Needless to say, they mean the same thing: to remove the backbone from a whole bird so that it can be flattened.

Butterflying a chicken is a fantastic technique, especially for busy home cooks. I honestly don't know why it isn't more popular. Doing it helps a whole chicken cook faster, more evenly, and yields a bird with juicier meat and crispier skin all over.

There's just one important thing to consider. When you plan to cook a butterflied chicken, stick with a bird that's three to four pounds. One that is much heavier will require a longer cooking time that mitigates the virtues of this technique.

1. Remove the backbone.

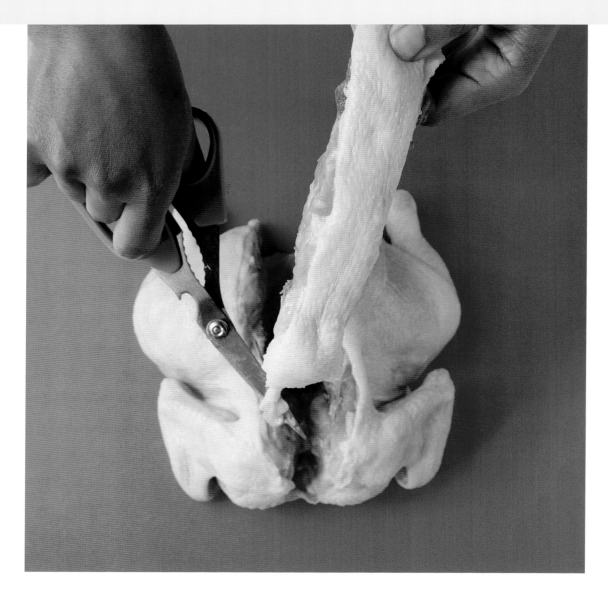

Place the chicken on your cutting board breast side down with the legs facing you. Use your kitchen shears to cut along one entire side of the backbone. Repeat on the other side, releasing the backbone completely.

2. Flatten the bird.

Flip the chicken over and open it up. Using your palms, press down on the breast to flatten the bird.

ROAST THAT BUTTERFLY

I love roasting butterflied chickens. This technique allows the chicken to roast in less time, plus the meat cooks and the skin crisps more evenly. Who's going to complain about that?!

HOW TO
Butterfly a Chicken Breast

You can also butterfly a boneless, skinless chicken breast. Though when working with this cut, you cannot call it spatchcocking. Sorry, but that excellence is saved only for the whole bird.

When you butterfly a boneless, skinless breast, you split it in half horizontally and open it like a book to make one much larger or two separate thinner cutlets.

Doing this approximately evens out the thickness of a chicken breast, but if you really want to ensure even thickness throughout, you should pound the cutlet before seasoning and cooking. To do this, lay the butterflied cutlet(s) flat in a plastic food storage bag or between two pieces of plastic wrap before pounding them with a meat mallet.

You'll want to butterfly the breast yourself — as opposed to buying cutlets at the market — anytime you cut up a whole chicken, whenever you can't find thin-sliced cutlets at the store, or if you just want to save money. Store-bought cutlets are usually significantly more expensive per pound.

1. Carefully slice the breast.

2. Open the split breast.

Place the chicken breast on your cutting board and hold it firmly in place with the palm of your non-dominant hand. Starting at the thickest part of the breast, slice it in half horizontally with one long, smooth slice of a chef's knife, being careful not to cut all the way through the other side.

Open the split breast like a book. It will look almost like a butterfly (hence the name!). I prefer to split the extra large cutlet in half down the middle to create two smaller, thinner cutlets (and do so for every recipe in this book). If the thickness of both resulting cutlets is fairly even, you're good to go. If not, pound them to an even thickness.

CHILL OUT

If you're having a hard time making a clean, smooth cut while butterflying a chicken breast, try putting it in the freezer for about 30 minutes. This will help firm up the meat and give you more control.

HOW TO
Carve a Whole Cooked Chicken

It's all well and good to know how to cut up raw chicken so that you can make the most of your bird, thereby saving money, but it's also important to know how to carve a whole chicken once it comes out of the oven. Because if nothing else, it makes you look good. It also helps reduce food waste, which is the more meaningful reason.

Before cutting into your delicious roast chicken, I implore you to let your bird rest for at least five minutes before carving. Honestly, ten minutes is ideal, but I know that you're hungry. This step is to make sure that your chicken retains its juices and stays moist.

Once it has rested, place your chicken on a cutting board. Ideally this board is different from the one that you use for cutting raw meat (see page 16) and has a groove to catch the juices that will inevitably run as you carve your bird.

1. Remove the wings.

2. Remove the leg quarters.

Remove the wings by gently pulling them away from the body to expose the wing joint. You may have to cut slightly into the breast to see it. Once you do, cut through the joint to detach the wing. Repeat on the other side.

(Sound familiar? Carving a cooked chicken is a lot like breaking down a raw one!)

Slice just enough between the leg and the body to be able to gently pull the leg away from the body and reveal the joint. Once you see it, cut through it. Repeat on the other side.

3. Split the leg quarters.

To separate the drumstick from the thigh, just cut through the joint. It's pretty easy to spot — it's at the angle.

4. Split and slice the breast.

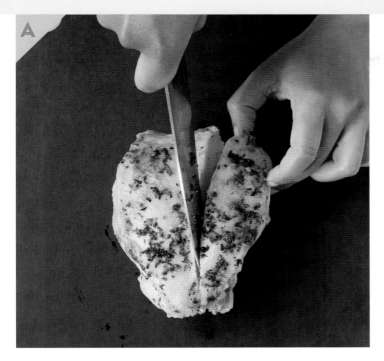

A | Place the breast on your cutting board skin side up and cut straight down one side of the breastbone, hugging the bone as closely as possible. Continue to follow the curvature even once you hit the wishbone; on the left side that will mean curving to the left and on the right side it will mean curving to the right.

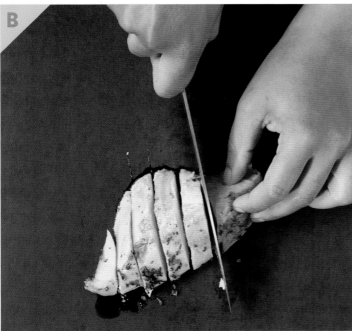

B | Once both breasts are free, place each on the cutting board, straighten the skin, if necessary, and slice them crosswise on the bias to get even slices.

PART 3
RECIPES

Authenticity, Tradition & Ease

THERE'S A LONG-OVERDUE CONVERSATION happening in the food world about authenticity and tradition, but it's tricky. What's authentic food in a country founded on the idea of being a melting pot? And how can we avoid using that question as an excuse to be thoughtless about inclusivity?

For example: I'm a first generation Greek-American whose grandmother cooked exclusively Greek food, but only the recipes she could remember from her region of Greece, with the ingredients she could get here in the States. Having been to Greece only six times myself, how much claim do I have to "authentic" Greek food? What about authentic Greek-American food? Is that even a thing?

It strikes me that those of us who create recipes and tell stories of food and culture must do so from an honest and deeply personal place. We must seek to learn about cultural traditions from people who have lived them firsthand, and when we play with culture, we must do so out of love and respect, with clear intention to our readers about why and how we are doing so.

With the charge of writing a whole cookbook about chicken, and as a person with a passion for travel and global cuisines, there was no way that I'd be able to keep from sharing recipes from cultures other than my own. I've tried to share only recipes with which I have personal ties and to share those experiences with you. I tried to be clear when I felt I understood the roots of a recipe, but keep in mind that I'm always adjusting to make recipes as easy as possible for busy American home cooks — thinking about what we have access to and how we tend to live, feed our children, and so on.

So with that, go forth and learn more. This book is by no means the be-all and end-all of anything except, well, chicken. My hope is that my Chicken Laarb (page 105), Sheet Pan Shawarma (page 67), and My Favorite Fast Food–Style Fried Chicken Sandwich (page 112), for example, encourage you to explore food with curiosity, respect, and a desire to learn from, cook with, and break bread with people from places you have not yet experienced or maybe just neighbors whose American experience is different from your own.

IN AN OVEN
Roasting & Baking

A simple roast chicken is the quintessential home-cooked meal. But while pulling a whole bird with crisped, lacquered skin out of the oven is certainly glorious, there is much more you can do with chicken using just your oven and a handful of fresh ingredients.

Whether you mix up a compound butter to simply roast your favorite chicken parts in a hurry or throw together a complete meal on a sheet pan, your oven can do the heavy lifting when you need to prep quickly and let cooking happen on its own.

ROASTING VERSUS BAKING

TECHNICALLY, ALL CHICKEN COOKED IN THE OVEN IS ROASTED. *Baked* is a term applied to foods that change form when cooked in the oven, such as a batter that goes from liquid to solid. But there's a lot of gray area in how these words are applied, and when a dish that's normally fried is cooked in the oven instead, like the chicken tenders in this chapter, it's typically described as baked. Some refer to any chicken that has been coated in flour and cooked in the oven as baked.

Of all the recipes in this book, the ones in this chapter are the least forgiving and also the ones that are the most gratifying to master, so having the right tools makes a big difference. Check out pages 20–21 to learn more about getting your hands on a roasting pan, compatible rack, and instant-read meat thermometer. Kitchen shears, too, if you want to butterfly your bird, which I highly recommend.

TO BRINE OR NOT TO BRINE?

SOMEONE COULD WRITE AN ENTIRE BOOK on the topic of brining alone. But I didn't. Nor do I desire to delve quite that deep into the science. I have a feeling that you might feel the same, though understanding the basics is pretty useful.

Here's what I think you should know.

Wet Brining

Wet brining is the act of soaking your bird in a salt-water solution to yield firmer, juicier chicken. You can brine any cut and any brand of chicken, though *Cook's Illustrated* recently found that air-chilled chickens fare better in wet brines than water-chilled birds, which aren't able to soak up as much salt from the brine (check out page 14 to learn more about the difference between air- and water-chilled chickens).

When making a wet brine, you can either use coarse kosher or regular fine table salt, though I prefer the latter because of how quickly it dissolves in liquid. Just keep in mind that if you come across a recipe that calls for coarser kosher salt and you want to substitute fine table salt, you'll have to cut the amount of salt in half.

To flavor your brine, you can add fresh herbs, garlic, and even sugar, which you'll come across most often in recipes for grilled meats. Herbs and garlic impart flavor; sugar, on the other hand, is about accelerating caramelization.

The downsides of making a wet brine are that it can be cumbersome to store (whatever big container you use to soak chicken in tons of salted water will have to stay in the refrigerator the whole time); leaving the meat in a wet brine too long can cause your chicken to get overly salty and even rob it of flavor (the chicken will soak up water as well as salt); and the brine can inhibit chicken skin from crisping (because it will saturate the skin with water).

.HOW TO MAKE A.
WET BRINE

You should always follow specific recipes, but here are guidelines for making a basic wet brine for chicken. As a rule of thumb, allow the chicken to sit for 1 hour.

FOR A WHOLE CHICKEN OR BONE-IN CHICKEN PIECES (up to 9 pounds): Use ½ cup fine table salt for every 8 cups of cold water.

FOR BONELESS, SKINLESS CHICKEN BREASTS (up to 6 pounds): Use ¼ cup fine table salt for every 8 cups of cold water.

WHAT ABOUT BUTTERMILK?

You may be wondering how a brine can inhibit chicken skin from crisping when so many fried chicken recipes call for a buttermilk brine. But, oh friends: no matter how you season it, buttermilk does not make a brine. Technically, brine can only be made with water.

The fats in buttermilk, which are not present in a proper brine, make it easier for a coating to stick to chicken skin, which is one of several reasons why a buttermilk *dip* or *soak* can be great for fried chicken. So alas, there is the answer — and also more proof on how a whole book could be written on the subject of brining. Any takers?

Dry Brining

Having made the point that a buttermilk brine is technically not a brine, I should mention that *dry brine* is a misnomer as well. Merriam-Webster defines the noun *brine* as "water saturated or strongly impregnated with common salt." Dry, of course, means that no water is involved, which, by the way, is why I prefer a dry brine — but more on that in a second.

To make a dry brine, you simply rub the chicken all over with salt and, if you want, other herbs and aromatics like lemon zest. The result is juicier, more tender meat and crispier skin. Though you'll end up with something similar to a wet brine, there is a subtle difference.

Where a wet brine will plump the meat but make it harder for the skin to crisp, a dry brine does the opposite. The salt rub helps the skin crisp and the chicken retain its juiciness without plumping the meat with water. And it's this difference, combined with the ease of a dry brine, that makes it my exclusive go-to for home cooking.

There's one last consideration when choosing between a wet and dry brine. Dry brines add flavor on the skin, but wet ones can lend flavor to the meat itself. That's why wet brines can be worth the trouble on Thanksgiving. Who doesn't want to bet on giving your turkey extra moisture and flavor when there's so much else — i.e., risk of *overcooking* — going on?

But for weeknight chicken? It doesn't make as much sense.

I've come across very few recipes calling for wet brines that are worth the trouble on a busy weeknight. None of the wet brines I experimented with for this book ended up being worth the extra time and effort. But if you come across a chicken recipe with an interesting-sounding wet brine, by all means, give it a go when you've got the time!

TRUSS ISSUES

A TELEVISION PRODUCER ONCE DISCOURAGED ME from featuring a whole chicken recipe on a live segment because "even top chefs mess up when trying to truss a bird on live TV."

Trussing a chicken correctly is hard. It's not just you. So here's the good news: it's not necessary.

I'm not just giving you a pass because you're a home cook. Keeping the legs open allows for increased hot air flow all around, making for better, more even cooking. And, no, your chicken won't dry out because you'll be stuffing your bird with citrus and other good stuff to help keep the meat moist and flavorful.

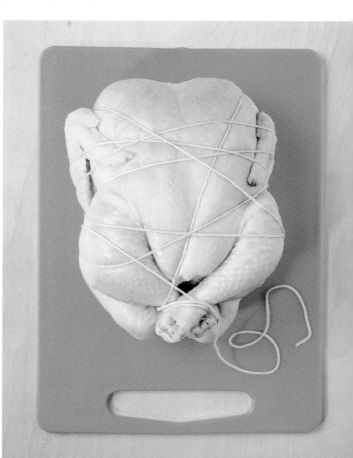

·HOW TO MAKE A.
DRY BRINE

Unlike a wet brine, a dry brine is very much worth the extra time, even on a weeknight, if you have it to spare — *especially* when roasting a chicken. In fact, I strongly advise that you plan ahead and salt your chicken the night before.

While a dry brine will benefit your bird even if it only has 1 hour to work, you'll be amazed at how juicy the meat and crispy the skin is if you dry brine it for 24 hours.

1 Pat the chicken dry with paper towels, including inside the emptied cavity.

2 Sprinkle the chicken generously with salt, all around the body and inside the cavity, too. Use 2 teaspoons of fine table salt or, if you have it, double that amount of coarse kosher salt for a 3½- to 4½-pound whole chicken or comparable amount of bone-in chicken parts. You can combine the salt with minced fresh herbs or dried herbs and spices. Aromatics like lemon zest make a lovely addition, too, depending on your final recipe.

3 Place a rack on top of a large sheet pan and rest the chicken on the rack. Place it in the refrigerator, uncovered, for at least 1 hour and ideally up to 24 hours, but not longer.

When it's time to cook your chicken, remove it from the refrigerator and, if there's time, allow it to come to room temperature before putting it in the oven.

Also — and this is important — if you have dry brined your bird, skip whatever salting your recipe calls for before cooking.

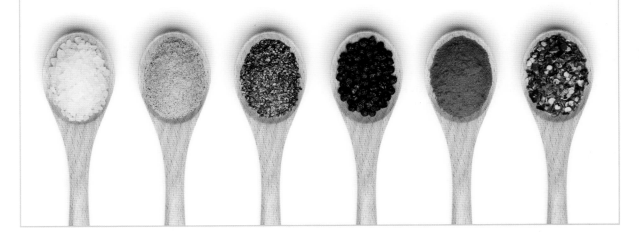

Crazy Delicious Classic Roast Chicken

4 servings

INGREDIENTS

- 1 whole chicken (3½ to 4 pounds)
- 1 large shallot, cut in half lengthwise
- 4 tablespoons unsalted butter, softened to room temperature
- 1 packed tablespoon finely chopped herbs of choice (such as rosemary, sage, thyme, or tarragon; I like to use a combination of all)
- 2 teaspoons salt
- 1 teaspoon freshly ground black pepper
- 1 lemon, quartered

COOK'S NOTES

Use a rack for crispy skin on the bottom.

If you have the time to dry brine, you won't regret it. Follow the directions on page 51 and skip the salt in this recipe.

My first (anxious) thought when I agreed to write this book was: How can I possibly come up with a new classic roast chicken recipe? But the more I researched, the more I realized that there's no "perfect" way to roast chicken.

Some say start at a high temp and then go low. Others say to roast low and slow the whole time. And so on. With that in mind, I boldly set out to make a crazy delicious roast chicken that is easily replicated by even the least experienced home cooks. I can't guarantee that this recipe is completely foolproof, but it's pretty close, especially if you use an instant-read thermometer.

1 If you have time, remove the chicken from your refrigerator up to 1 hour before cooking. When ready to cook, preheat the oven to 450°F (230°C) and make the herb butter: Dice half of the shallot to yield 1½ to 2 tablespoons; set aside the other half without chopping. In a small bowl, use a fork to mash together the butter, diced shallot, and herbs; set aside.

2 Pat the chicken dry with paper towels, including inside the cavity. Sprinkle the chicken with the salt and pepper, dividing them evenly all over the body and putting some inside the cavity as well.

3 Rub roughly two-thirds of the herb butter all over the chicken, including under the skin and inside the cavity; set the remaining one-third of the herb butter aside. Cut the remaining half shallot into two or three pieces lengthwise, and stuff them inside the cavity along with the quartered lemon.

4 Put the chicken breast side up on a rack set in a roasting pan and place the pan in the oven. If you want to set a master timer for your overall cooking time, do so now for 60 minutes.

After the chicken has cooked for 15 minutes, spread the remaining herb butter all over the exposed chicken skin, getting it into as many nooks and crannies between the legs, wings, and body as possible.

After another 15 minutes, baste the chicken with drippings and reduce the oven temperature to 400°F (200°C).

5 Continue roasting for another 30 minutes, basting at least two more times. If at any point the drippings begin to burn, add a big splash of water to the bottom of the pan. After 60 minutes total cook time, check for doneness: an instant-read thermometer should register 160°F (70°C) at the thickest part of the breast and 165°F (75°C) at the thigh. If the chicken is not cooked through, roast for 5 to 10 minutes longer until it is.

6 Allow the chicken to rest for ideally 10 minutes before serving.

·BUTTERS FOR A·
BETTER BIRD

Now that's a slogan I can get behind! Allow me to introduce you to my favorite culinary hat trick: compound butter.

Compound butter is unsalted butter that is traditionally flavored with fresh herbs; some form of onion, garlic, or shallots; and aromatic ingredients. But really, you can add anything from lemon zest to freshly squeezed citrus juice, finely minced chipotles to maple syrup. You can even make strawberry-basil butter by using strawberry preserves and fresh basil. The possibilities are truly endless.

1 Start by bringing the unsalted butter just to room temperature; you should be able to mash it by hand, but it shouldn't be *too* soft.

2 In the meantime, finely mince or grate all of the other ingredients you plan to incorporate. Then use a fork to mix the softened butter with everything, adding some salt (I like to use about ¼ teaspoon of fine sea salt for every ½ cup of butter).

3 Once all of the ingredients are evenly incorporated, spoon the butter onto parchment paper and roll it into a neat log. Wrap tightly, twisting the ends of the paper to seal, and refrigerate for at least 3 hours before using. The butter will keep in the refrigerator for up to 7 days or in the freezer for up to 3 months.

I could give you general measurements — for example, use 2 tablespoons of chopped fresh herbs for every ½ cup of butter — but I'm always breaking my own rules. While you'll find that I used exactly this amount for the butter in my Crazy Delicious Classic Roast Chicken recipe (page 53), I ended up using much more fresh cilantro to make the butter for my Jalapeño Roasted Chicken with Cilantro Butter (page 56). Just because more cilantro is more better. Basically, compound butter is forgiving, and you should taste as you go.

Here are a few of my favorite flavor combinations for chicken:

- Lemon, capers, and fresh dill
- Sautéed or raw shallot, Dijon mustard, and fresh tarragon
- Garlic, Parmesan cheese, and black pepper
- Chipotles, the adobo sauce they're packed in, orange zest, and maple syrup
- Miso, fresh chopped scallion, grated ginger, and chili paste

INGREDIENTS

- 1 whole chicken (3½ to 4 pounds)

- 4 tablespoons unsalted butter, softened to room temperature

- ¼ cup finely chopped fresh cilantro

- 1 teaspoon minced or grated garlic (from 1 large or 2 small cloves)

- 2 teaspoons salt

- 1 teaspoon freshly ground black pepper

- 3 fresh jalapeños, trimmed and split in half lengthwise

- ¼ of a large orange, cut into 2 small pieces

COOK'S NOTES

Use a rack for crispy skin on the bottom.

If you have the time to dry brine, you won't regret it. Follow the directions on page 51 and skip the salt in this recipe.

Don't worry about all those jalapeños stuffed into the cavity — they help keep the meat moist and lend just a hint of their bright flavor without giving heat. I like making this chicken for when I want leftovers to use in other Mexican dishes or quick and easy Tex-Mex weeknight pleasers like quesadillas, tacos, or tostadas.

Jalapeño Roasted Chicken *with Cilantro Butter*

Here's the thing about my approach to roast chicken: Once you know how to make the classic, you pretty much know how to make 1,001 versions. Because the trick to making it delicious is compound butter (page 54) — and once you know how to make one compound butter, you know how to make them all.

Given that my Crazy Delicious Classic Roast Chicken (page 53) is nothing more than a bird sprinkled with salt and pepper, slathered with compound butter, and stuffed with a few ingredients to help keep it juicy, you can see how easy it is to riff on the recipe. And that's what I did here, using my favorite Mexican ingredients.

1 If you have time, remove the chicken from your refrigerator up to 1 hour before cooking. When ready to cook, preheat the oven to 450°F (230°C) and make the herb butter: In a small bowl, use a fork to mash together the butter, cilantro, and garlic; set aside.

2 Pat the chicken dry with paper towels, including inside the cavity. Sprinkle the chicken with the salt and pepper, dividing them evenly all over the body and putting some inside the cavity as well.

3 Rub roughly two-thirds of the herb butter all over the chicken, including under the skin and inside the cavity; set the remaining one-third of the herb butter aside. Stuff the jalapeños and orange pieces inside the cavity.

4 Put the chicken breast side up on a rack set in a roasting pan and place the pan in the oven. If you want to set a master timer for your overall cooking time, do so now for 60 minutes.

After the chicken has cooked for 15 minutes, spread the remaining herb butter all over the exposed chicken skin, getting into as many nooks and crannies between the legs, wings, and body as possible.

After another 15 minutes, baste the chicken with drippings and reduce the oven temperature to 400°F (200°C).

5 Continue roasting for another 30 minutes, basting at least two more times. If at any point the drippings begin to burn, add a big splash of water to the bottom of the pan. After 60 minutes total cook time, check for doneness: an instant-read thermometer should register 160°F (70°C) at the thickest part of the breast and 165°F (75°C) at the thigh. If the chicken is not cooked through, roast for 5 to 10 minutes longer until it is.

6 Allow the chicken to rest for ideally 10 minutes before serving.

There's no reason dinner should have you running around like, well, a chicken with its head cut off. For most, weeknight cooking needs to be fast and easy, which is why many rule out roast chicken. But as you can see from the recipes in this chapter, the oven can be your friend, even on Monday through Thursday nights. If you want a whole roasted bird done in a jiff, though, the key is to butterfly it (page 33) and keep the seasoning simple.

If you have time, dry brine a 3- to 4-pound chicken at least 1 hour before cooking or, ideally, as long as overnight. You can do this before or after you butterfly it — whatever makes most sense for you. Try to return the chicken to room temperature before cooking.

When ready to cook, gently pat the bird dry with paper towels and season it all over with 2 tablespoons of olive oil and 1 teaspoon of freshly ground black pepper. Preheat the oven to 425°F (220°C), place the chicken skin side up in a roasting pan or on a sheet pan, and roast for about 35 minutes. Baste with drippings a few times throughout cooking, and check for doneness before pulling the chicken out for good. It is done when an instant-read thermometer registers 160°F (70°C) at the thickest part of the breast and 165°F (75°C) at the thigh. Allow it to rest for 5 to 10 minutes before serving.

Voilà: dinner's ready.

FIVE ALL-PURPOSE SAUCES
for Dipping, Dressing, and Drizzling

ONE

Tzatziki
Makes 1 cup

A go-to in my house, this cucumber-yogurt sauce can be whipped up in five minutes. And psst: if you're in a rush, measurements hardly matter. It's hard to go wrong and easy to adjust. Sometimes I add fresh dill, too.

- ¾ cup plain Greek-style yogurt (about one 5.3- to 6-ounce container)
- ¼ cup finely diced, seeded cucumber
- 1 small garlic clove, minced or grated
- 1 tablespoon lemon juice (from about ½ a juicy lemon)
- 1 teaspoon olive oil
- ¼ teaspoon salt

Combine all of the ingredients in a bowl and mix well. Adjust the seasoning to taste. Serve immediately or store in the refrigerator for up to 5 days.

TWO

Chimichurri
Makes ½ cup

You'll find nearly as many versions of chimichurri as you will homes in Argentina, this sauce's place of origin, so feel free to play with your favorite herbs or whichever ones you happen to have on hand. Spoon this over nearly any roasted or grilled meat, especially chicken, to guarantee a winning dinner.

- ½ cup fresh cilantro, finely chopped
- ½ cup flat-leaf parsley leaves, finely chopped
- ¼ cup very finely chopped red onion
- 2 tablespoons finely chopped fresh mint (optional)
- 2 tablespoons red wine vinegar
- ¼ teaspoon salt
- ¼ teaspoon red pepper flakes
- 3 tablespoons high-quality olive oil

Combine all of the ingredients except for the oil in a bowl and mix together. Pour the oil on top and stir to combine well. Adjust the seasoning to taste. Serve immediately or store in the refrigerator for up to 7 days.

THREE

Lebanese Garlic Sauce

Makes 1¼ cups

Much like a childhood favorite of mine — a Greek garlic-and-potato spread called skordalia — toum, as the Lebanese version is called, is an unforgettably delicious creamy, white, pungent sauce with a pure garlic flavor. It's a bit easier to make (no potatoes!) and works better as a sauce and spread for meat (skordalia is more of a mezze dip). Slather it on my Sheet Pan Shawarma (page 67) or any chicken that you tuck into pita sandwiches.

½ cup whole garlic cloves, about 20 cloves (from about 2 small heads), peeled and trimmed

¾ teaspoon salt

4 tablespoons lemon juice (from about 2 juicy lemons)

1½ cups neutral oil, such as grapeseed or canola

1 Add the garlic and salt to a food processor. Pulse, scraping down the sides occasionally, until finely minced.

2 With the motor running, very slowly add the lemon juice in a thin, steady stream. You may have to stop halfway, and again once all of the juice has been added, to scrape down the sides. A paste should begin to form.

3 With the motor running, very slowly add the oil in a thin, steady stream, stopping periodically to scrape down the sides, especially early on in the process. Toward the end, you should find that the mixture is emulsifying, i.e., turning into a consistency similar to thick mayonnaise, which is the goal.

Adjust the seasoning to taste, as it may vary depending on the sharpness of your fresh garlic; you can add a little ice-cold water to mellow the flavor. If you do this, add it as you did the lemon juice and oil: in a thin, steady stream with the motor of the food processor running the whole time. Just be mindful not to add too much additional liquid, whether water or lemon juice, or you risk messing with the consistency.

FOUR

Zingy Roasted Red Pepper Sauce
Makes 1 cup

I came up with this lovely sauce years ago to lure my younger son from ketchup, the attraction to which was the bright red color. This substitute (which worked!) is as basic as it gets, but even tastier and more fun to play with.

Feel free to add a few leaves of basil or a small handful of toasted walnuts (both together would be nice). Add the shallot and garlic, or stick with just one. Lemon juice or sherry vinegar go nicely as a substitute for red wine vinegar, too.

    1 (12-ounce) jar roasted red peppers, drained

    1 tablespoon olive oil

    2½ teaspoons red wine vinegar

    2 teaspoons minced shallot (from about ¼ of a shallot) and/or 1 garlic clove, roughly chopped (see headnote)

    ½ teaspoon salt

Combine all of the ingredients in a blender or food processor and pulse until you reach the desired consistency. Adjust the seasoning to taste. Serve immediately or store in the refrigerator for up to 7 days.

COOK'S NOTE

If you purée this longer and add additional liquid — from the jar of roasted red peppers plus a little extra vinegar — you can make a thinner sauce to toss with pasta on nights when you don't want chicken. If you can imagine that.

FIVE

Peanut Sauce
Makes 1 to 1½ cups

Peanut sauce is one of the most versatile things that you can keep in your refrigerator. You can use it to marinate chunks of boneless, skinless chicken breast to grill on skewers, as a dipping sauce for roast chicken, or to toss with noodles and shredded poached chicken for a nearly instant dinner. And that's just the beginning.

The yield of this sauce will vary greatly depending on how thick you make it, which depends on how you want to use it. For a dressing or marinade, make it thinner, but keep it thick for a dipping sauce. Adjust the thickness by the amount of water you add and, if using a high-powered blender, also by how long you allow the blender to run (the longer it goes, the thinner the sauce will get).

    ½ cup unsweetened peanut butter

    2 tablespoons hoisin sauce

    1½ tablespoons chopped fresh chives (you can substitute 1 tablespoon chopped scallion, green part only)

    1 tablespoon lime juice (from about ½ a juicy lime), plus more to taste

    2 teaspoons pure maple syrup

    1–1½ teaspoons minced or grated fresh ginger, depending on how much bite you want

    1 teaspoon toasted sesame oil, plus more for additional sesame flavor

Combine all of the ingredients in a blender and, starting on low, blend, adding room-temperature water in small amounts. As the sauce smooths out, slowly crank up the power to help it come along, scraping down the sides occasionally. For a thicker sauce, like a dip, add about ¼ cup plus 2 tablespoons of water. For a thinner dressing, add up to ¼ cup of water, plus up to an additional 2 tablespoons lime juice.

Oliver's Chicken

4 servings

INGREDIENTS

- 1 whole chicken (3 to 4 pounds), butter-flied (page 33)
- 1½ pounds new potatoes
- 2 tablespoons olive oil, plus more as needed
- 2 tablespoons lemon juice (from about 1 juicy lemon)
- 3 teaspoons salt
- 1 teaspoon garlic powder
- 1 teaspoon freshly ground black pepper
- 1 (14-ounce) can artichoke bottoms, drained and quartered (you can substitute halved artichoke hearts)
- 1 cup small, pitted green olives, such as Manzanilla

COOK'S NOTE

If you have the time to dry brine, you won't regret it. Follow the directions on page 51 and skip the salt in this recipe.

Truth time: This isn't just Oliver's chicken. There's a little bit of inspiration from everyone in my family in this dish, but it was easy to name the recipe after my youngest son because of all the olives. He's also the most fickle about meat, but this dinner is always a sure thing with him.

1 If you have time, remove the chicken from your refrigerator up to 1 hour before cooking. When ready to cook, preheat the oven to 425°F (200°C) and prep the potatoes: Cut the potatoes in half. Add them to a medium bowl with the oil, 1 tablespoon of the lemon juice, 1 teaspoon of the salt, and the garlic powder. Toss to coat well and transfer to a shallow roasting pan or a large sheet pan.

Set the bowl, which should still have a little bit of the oil–lemon juice mixture at the bottom, aside.

2 Pat the chicken dry with paper towels, and season it with the remaining 2 teaspoons salt and the pepper, dividing them evenly between both sides of the chicken.

Nestle the chicken skin side up between all of the potatoes on the roasting pan, making sure that the potatoes remain in a single layer and that none get stuck under the bird. Pour the remaining oil–lemon juice mixture from the bowl onto the chicken and rub it into the skin.

3 Place the pan in the oven and cook for 30 minutes, basting the chicken with drippings and shaking the potatoes every 10 minutes or so. If at any point there aren't enough drippings to baste the bird, drizzle a small amount of oil onto the chicken and use that.

After 30 minutes, baste the chicken with the remaining 1 tablespoon lemon juice. Add the artichoke bottoms and olives to the pan, scattering them all around the bird.

Cook for another 5 minutes before checking for doneness: an instant-read thermometer should register 160°F (70°C) at the thickest part of the breast and 165°F (75°C) at the thigh. If the chicken is not cooked through, roast for 5 to 10 minutes longer until it is.

4 Allow the chicken to rest for ideally 10 minutes before serving.

Baked Cacio e Pepe Chicken Tenders

4 servings

INGREDIENTS

- Cooking spray
- ½ cup all-purpose flour
- 3 eggs
- 2 cups panko breadcrumbs
- ½ cup grated Parmesan or Grana Padano
- ½ cup grated Pecorino cheese
- 3 tablespoons olive oil
- 1½ teaspoons freshly ground black pepper
- 1 teaspoon salt
- 1½ pounds boneless, skinless chicken breasts, cut into 2-inch-thick strips

COOK'S NOTES

You can use a full cup of Parmesan, Grana Padano, Pecorino, or even Romano instead of the combination of cheeses.

For more traditional chicken tenders, use ½ cup Parmesan or Grana Padano and just ½ to 1 teaspoon of black pepper. Add other spices like dried oregano, paprika, or garlic powder as desired. Serve with honey mustard or BBQ dipping sauce.

Everyone loves crispy chicken tenders. This, I believe, is a fact of life. And the good news is that they can be made easily, and even fairly healthfully, in the oven. The key to getting tenders as crispy as fried without dunking them in hot oil is to toss the breadcrumbs in a bit of oil before coating the chicken. Then, bake at high heat.

When making chicken tenders, I'm always playing with flavor to come up with something that appeals to my kids and also feels a little more grown-up for me. This recipe was inspired by one of my favorite pasta dishes, which is great topped with grilled chicken.

1 Preheat the oven to 450°F (230°C). Line a large sheet pan with aluminum foil for easy cleanup and place a rack on top. Spray the rack with cooking spray and set aside.

Set up your coating station: Add the flour to a wide, shallow bowl. Crack the eggs into a separate wide, shallow bowl and whisk. Add the breadcrumbs, cheeses, oil, pepper, and salt to a third wide, shallow bowl and, using your hands, toss to combine well, making sure that all of the breadcrumbs get evenly coated with oil.

2 Dredge all of the chicken strips in flour, shaking each piece to remove excess before setting aside. (I find it least messy to complete the flour step before moving on to the egg dip.)

3 One by one, dip each floured chicken strip into the egg, coating it completely, and then into the seasoned breadcrumbs, pressing down to help the breadcrumbs stick. Place the breaded strips on the prepared baking rack and repeat until they are all coated.

4 Bake the chicken strips in the oven for about 12 minutes, until cooked through, flipping halfway through the cooking time. If you find that the chicken isn't crisping up as much as you'd like, give them a light coating of cooking spray for the last half of the cooking time. Serve immediately.

Sheet Pan Shawarma

4 servings

INGREDIENTS

- ¼ cup plus 1½ tablespoons olive oil
- ¼ cup lemon juice (from about 2 juicy lemons)
- 3 large garlic cloves, finely minced or grated
- 1 tablespoon ground cumin
- 2 teaspoons minced or grated fresh ginger
- 2 teaspoons ground turmeric
- 2 teaspoons ground coriander
- ½ teaspoon smoked or sweet paprika (or a combination)
- ½ teaspoon freshly ground black pepper
- ⅛ teaspoon ground cinnamon
- 2 pounds boneless, skinless chicken thighs
- 2 small or 1 extra-large red onion, peeled, trimmed, and cut into 1-inch-thick wedges
- 1 pint cherry tomatoes
- 1 teaspoon salt
- Fresh parsley, for garnish (optional)
- Warmed pita bread, for serving

For my kids, growing up half Greek in Brooklyn, anything that comes wrapped in flatbread is pretty much comfort food. While there's a difference between Greek gyro and Middle Eastern shawarma — and even variations between Turkish and Lebanese shawarma, for example — at home I play with and combine variations. I encourage you to do the same while exploring flavors and cultures, too.

Sometimes I serve this with Tzatziki (page 59) and other times with Lebanese Garlic Sauce (page 60). If you're in a super rush, you can whisk tahini with water to just shy of the desired thickness. Then add a tablespoon of olive oil and lemon juice to taste. Need to go even faster? Throw your favorite store-bought hummus on the table for the spreading.

1 In a medium bowl, whisk together the ¼ cup oil, the lemon juice, garlic, cumin, ginger, turmeric, coriander, paprika, pepper, and cinnamon. Add the chicken and, using your clean hands or tongs, toss to coat well. Cover and leave at room temperature to marinate for 30 to 60 minutes, or place in the refrigerator for up to 2 hours.

2 When ready to cook, preheat the oven to 375°F (190°C).
Place the onion wedges in a medium bowl along with the tomatoes, the remaining 1½ tablespoons oil, and the salt. Toss to coat well, and transfer to a sheet pan.

3 Nestle the chicken between all of the vegetables on the sheet pan, making sure that the vegetables remain in a single layer and that none get stuck under the chicken. Place the sheet pan in the oven and cook for 30 minutes. (This is a good time to make a sauce, if desired; see the headnote.)

4 Remove the sheet pan from the oven and turn the broiler to high. Carefully transfer the chicken to a cutting board and slice it into ¼- to ½-inch-wide strips. Pour any accumulated juices from the sheet pan into a heatproof measuring cup; set aside. Transfer the sliced chicken back onto the sheet pan.

5 Place the sheet pan under the broiler for about 5 minutes, until everything chars in spots. Remove the sheet pan from the oven and spoon some of the reserved juices over the chicken and veggies to keep them moist. Season to taste one final time with salt and pepper, and garnish with parsley, if desired. Serve immediately with warmed pita and sauce of choice, if using.

INGREDIENTS

FOR THE CHICKEN

- 2 tablespoons chili powder
- 1 tablespoon garlic powder
- 2 teaspoons salt
- 2 teaspoons ground cumin
- 3 bell peppers, cut into 1-inch-thick strips (I like using 1 red, 1 green, and 1 yellow or orange pepper)
- 1 large red onion, peeled, trimmed, and cut into ½-inch-thick wedges
- 3 tablespoons neutral oil, such as grapeseed
- 2 pounds boneless, skinless chicken breasts, cut into 1½- to 2-inch-thick strips
- Warmed tortillas, for serving
- Fresh cilantro, for serving (optional)
- Hot sauce, for serving (optional)

FOR THE LIME CREMA

- 1 cup sour cream
- 2 tablespoons lime juice (see headnote)
- ¼ teaspoon salt

Sheet Pan Fajitas
with Lime Crema

The only thing that makes me happier than fajitas is an easy cleanup meal. Bring the two together, like in this recipe, and I'm one happy cook. And that's even without the lime crema, which I can eat by the spoonful.

This is one of those rare times when bottled lime juice — with nothing added — is better than freshly squeezed. The reliable acidity level of bottled juice gives the sour cream an intensity that I love for this dish.

If you can't find bottled or prefer not to use it, you'll need one really juicy lime to get 2 tablespoons of juice — and more if the limes at your market are rock hard, which they tend to be many months of the year.

If freshly squeezed juice isn't giving you the punch of flavor that you want, don't add more juice, which will just thin the sour cream. Add lime zest instead.

1 **MAKE THE CHICKEN:** Preheat the oven to 400°F (200°C). In the meantime, combine the chili powder, garlic powder, salt, and cumin in a small bowl; set aside.

2 Combine the bell peppers, onion, and 2 tablespoons of the oil in a large bowl, along with about half of the spice mixture (about 3 tablespoons, though it's okay to estimate here). Toss to coat well and transfer the vegetables to a sheet pan.

3 Add the chicken strips to the same large bowl along with the remaining 1 tablespoon oil and remaining spice mixture. Toss to coat well and transfer the chicken to the sheet pan, arranging everything in a single layer as much as possible.

4 Place the sheet pan in the oven and cook for about 12 minutes, until the chicken is cooked through and the vegetables just begin to brown in spots. Turn the broiler to low and transfer the pan to the broiler for 5 to 7 minutes, until everything browns in spots.

If you prefer your veggies *charred* in spots, turn the broiler to high instead and cook for no more than 5 minutes, watching carefully to ensure that nothing burns too quickly and that the chicken doesn't overcook.

5 **MAKE THE LIME CREMA:** While the chicken is cooking, mix together the sour cream, lime juice, and salt in a medium serving bowl. Adjust the seasoning to taste; if using fresh lime juice, see the headnote about adding lime zest.

Serve the chicken and veggies with lime crema, warmed tortillas, fresh cilantro, and hot sauce, if desired.

CHOOSING YOUR CHEESE

I rarely come home from the market without a ball of fresh mozzarella cheese. It's a favorite ingredient in my house and, though I use it for the following dish from time to time, I have to admit that a good, old-fashioned block of supermarket mozzarella works really well in the recipe. It lends a saltier bite and the texture holds up better. I know — it surprised me, too!

Another fantastic option: Skip melting the cheese altogether and after the chicken is cooked through, drain the excess juices, tear into a big ball of fresh burrata cheese, and dot it all around the sheet pan. (You can do this with superfresh mozzarella as well.) Serve immediately and watch dinner go down!

Caprese Sheet Pan Chicken

4 servings

INGREDIENTS

- 2 pints cherry tomatoes
- 1 tablespoon olive oil
- 1 teaspoon salt
- 2 garlic cloves
- 9 large basil leaves
- ½ teaspoon lemon zest (from about ½ a washed lemon)
- 2 pounds boneless, skinless chicken breasts
- Freshly ground black pepper
- 8 ounces mozzarella cheese, sliced (about 2 slices per chicken breast)
- Crusty bread, for serving (optional)

COOK'S NOTE

Chiffonade — the French word for "ribbons" — sounds fancy, but it is a simple way of cutting leafy herbs, such as basil, into thin strips so that nobody ends up with an unwieldy piece.

Simply stack the large leaves on top of each other and roll them tightly into a log. Using a sharp knife, slice the leaves perpendicular to the roll. And you're done.

Chicken Parmesan is a childhood favorite of mine, but it's a pretty straightforward dish that's also very labor intensive and seriously heavy. That's why I decided to do something playful instead of traditional with my cheese-stuffed Chicken Parmesan Meatballs (page 95). Still, they didn't feel like quite enough.

This recipe — a lighter, healthier, and *easier* version of chicken Parm — was born to fill the void. It's especially great in the summer but lovely all year 'round. And it's delicious enough that I think it's becoming a childhood favorite for my own kids.

1. Preheat the oven to 400°F (200°C). Place the tomatoes on a sheet pan. Drizzle them with the oil, sprinkle with ½ teaspoon of the salt, and roll them around to coat evenly. Roast the tomatoes in the oven for 10 minutes.

2. In the meantime, prepare an herb paste for the chicken: Begin by roughly chopping the garlic and placing it in a pile on your cutting board. Roll up six of the basil leaves and place them on top of the pile of chopped garlic. Sprinkle with the remaining ½ teaspoon salt and the lemon zest, and chop everything together until the garlic, basil, salt, and zest turn into a rough paste. To help the process along, you can smash the leaves with the side of your knife from time to time. Set the herb paste aside.

3. Pat the chicken breasts dry on both sides with paper towels, and season generously with pepper.

By now, the tomatoes should be out of the oven. Nestle the chicken between the tomatoes on the pan, making sure to keep everything in a single layer. Spread the herb paste on top of each chicken breast, dividing it equally between them. Return the pan to the oven for 18 to 20 minutes, depending on the thickness of the chicken breasts.

4. Remove the sheet pan from the oven and turn the broiler to low. Top each chicken breast with mozzarella (two slices per breast works nicely) and place the entire pan under the broiler for 4 to 5 minutes. The cheese should melt and the tomatoes should char in spots. Watch carefully to ensure that nothing burns.

5. In the meantime, cut the remaining three basil leaves into chiffonade. Remove the pan from the broiler, garnish with the fresh basil, and serve immediately with crusty bread, if desired.

IN A PAN
Sautéing, Stir-Frying & Braising

There are myriad ways to cook chicken on your stovetop, and the cooking method you choose depends on two things: the cut of meat you're working with and what cookware you have available. Since we're mostly focused on simple, fresh, easy chicken dinners, we're going to keep our cookware choices limited. (The good news is that this doesn't limit our dinner options.) To cook anything in this book on the stovetop, you only need a big pot and two pans: a skillet and a sauté pan.

A skillet is a shallow pan that has sides that flare outward as they come up. A sauté pan is deeper and has straight sides. The difference, ironically, makes a skillet better for sautéing and a sauté pan better for shallow frying or dishes with a sauce.

INGREDIENTS

- 8 bone-in, skin-on chicken thighs (about 3½ to 4 pounds)
- 1½ teaspoons salt
- 1½ teaspoons freshly ground black pepper
- 2 tablespoons unsalted butter
- ¼ cup pure maple syrup
- ½ cup apple cider vinegar
- 1 cup thinly sliced shallots (from about 3 shallots)

FOR THE SLAW

- 1 large fennel bulb, trimmed, halved, and cored
- 1 Honeycrisp apple, halved and cored
- 2 tablespoons lemon juice (from about 1 juicy lemon)
- 1 tablespoon olive oil
- Salt

COOK'S NOTE

If you have the time to dry brine, you won't regret it. Follow the directions on page 51 and skip the salt in this recipe.

Chicken Thighs *with Maple–Cider Vinegar Glaze and Fennel–Apple Slaw*

I start this dish by cooking chicken thighs using a technique (page 75) that you can use for so many recipes, not just this one. But still: start by making this recipe as is. If you don't love the glaze, I at least guarantee that you'll make chicken thighs this way forever more.

(But seriously, if you don't love the glaze, hit me up on social media and let's talk. I'm here to help.)

1 If you have time, remove the chicken from your refrigerator up to 30 minutes before cooking. When ready to cook, pat the chicken dry with paper towels and season it with the salt and 1 teaspoon of the pepper, evenly dividing them between both sides of all the thighs.

2 Melt 1 tablespoon of the butter in a large heavy skillet set over medium-high heat. As soon as the foam subsides, add the chicken skin side down, making sure to press it as flat as possible onto the hot surface. Cook for 15 minutes, untouched, then flip and cook for another 15 minutes, untouched.

3 Melt the remaining 1 tablespoon butter in a medium saucepan set over medium-low heat. Add the maple syrup and cook until it just begins to bubble, about 2 minutes. (If the glaze takes fewer than 2 minutes to bubble, reduce the heat.) Add the vinegar and the remaining ½ teaspoon pepper. Continue to simmer the glaze on low for about 15 minutes, until it reduces to roughly ½ cup. Remove from the heat and set aside.

4 When the chicken is done cooking, transfer it to a plate. Drain the excess fat from the skillet and return to the stove over medium heat. Add the shallots and sauté until soft and fragrant, 1 to 2 minutes. Add the glaze to the skillet and use a wooden spoon or silicone spatula to scrape up the crispy bits. Cook for about 1 minute before returning the chicken to the skillet, skin side up, along with any accumulated juices.

5 Reduce the heat to medium-low and cook for 5 minutes longer. During the last minute of cooking, spoon the glaze over the thighs to lightly lacquer the skin. Turn the heat off and allow the chicken to rest for 5 minutes before serving.

6 **MAKE THE SLAW:** While the chicken rests, thinly slice the fennel and apple. Add both to a medium bowl and toss with the lemon juice, oil, and a pinch of salt, or to taste. Serve the chicken with more glaze spooned over the top and slaw on the side.

THE 30-MINUTE METHOD TO PERFECT THIGHS

If only this were a fitness book instead of a cookbook. But, alas, we can't have it all.

The way that we cook the bone-in, skin-on chicken thighs to make my Chicken Thighs with Maple–Cider Vinegar Glaze (page 74) is my method for cooking bone-in, skin-on chicken thighs on the stove in general. It's my go-to method whether I want sauce or not, whether I have only 30 minutes or a whole hour, whether I'm craving crispy skinned chicken seasoned only with salt and pepper or a more adventurous spice blend.

The technique is not my own; I discovered it in *Cooking by Hand* by Paul Bertolli. He described laying chicken down in a hot pan for 30 minutes, skin side down first, flipping it only once, pressing it down to create as much contact with the hot pan as possible, and otherwise leaving it untouched.

The untouched part is what got me. It sounded easy for a technique that would yield something cooked so perfectly. And it is.

Many other cooks have riffed on this master recipe, and I think that you should, too. Have a favorite spice blend? Sprinkle it on and give this method a try. Made some compound butter (page 54)? Finish your thighs off with a couple of tablespoons. Love making pan sauces? Cook up crispy thighs and go crazy with the drippings and crispy bits.

Even if your experiment leaves room for improvement, you can at least be sure that you'll end up with juicy, well-cooked chicken with supremely crispy skin.

And that's never bad.

Chicken Saltimbocca

4 servings

INGREDIENTS

2 pounds boneless, skinless chicken breasts, butter-flied (page 36, or use store-bought cutlets)

1½ teaspoons salt

1 teaspoon freshly ground black pepper

½ cup all-purpose flour

4 tablespoons unsalted butter

2 tablespoons olive oil, plus more as needed

Fresh sage leaves

¼ cup grated Parmesan cheese

¼ pound very thinly sliced prosciutto

3 garlic cloves, minced

¼ cup white wine

½ cup chicken stock (homemade, page 99, or store-bought)

¼ cup lemon juice (from about 2 juicy lemons)

Growing up in New Jersey meant growing up on simple Italian-American dishes, many of them served in the humble back dining rooms of pizzerias. They may not have looked like much by neighboring NYC restaurant standards, but some mighty delicious food came out of those kitchens. And it's in those locally owned, neighborhood restaurants where I learned about dishes like chicken saltimbocca.

1 Pat the chicken dry with paper towels and season with the salt and pepper, evenly dividing them between both sides of all the cutlets. Add the flour to a medium, shallow bowl and dredge the cutlets in the flour, shaking off excess before setting the cutlets aside.

2 Add 2 tablespoons of the butter and the oil to a large heavy skillet set over medium heat. As soon as the foam subsides, add the cutlets in a single layer (you may have to do this in batches). Place two or three sage leaves on top of each cutlet — however many fit without overlapping — and sprinkle with the Parmesan, dividing it equally among all of the cutlets. Top the sage leaves and Parm with a slice or two of prosciutto, pressing down on the prosciutto with a spatula. Cook for 3 minutes.

3 Carefully flip the cutlets and press down on them, helping the Parmesan cheese melt so that the prosciutto can adhere to the chicken. Cook for 3 to 4 minutes before transferring the cutlets to a plate, prosciutto side up.

If you have to cook your cutlets in batches, note that you may need to add an extra drizzle of oil and slightly reduce the heat to prevent burning, which may impact cooking time for the second batch.

4 Add the remaining 2 tablespoons butter and the garlic to the hot skillet. Cook until fragrant, about 1 minute. Add the wine and reduce by half, about 1 minute. Add the stock and bring to a boil. Reduce the heat to medium-low (or whatever heat allows you to maintain a gentle simmer), and reduce the sauce by half again, 3 to 4 minutes. Add the lemon juice and return the chicken to the pan, prosciutto side up, along with accumulated juices. Cook for 2 minutes longer, and serve immediately with sauce spooned over the top.

INGREDIENTS

FOR THE CHUTNEY

- 3 tablespoons unsalted butter
- 3 shallots, halved and thinly sliced
- 1 cup very finely chopped pitted prunes (from 12-ounce package)
- ½ cup dark brown or light brown sugar
- ¾ teaspoon Dijon mustard
- ½ cup apple cider vinegar
- ½ teaspoon salt
- Pinch of cinnamon

FOR THE CHICKEN

- 2 pounds boneless, skinless chicken breasts, butterflied (page 36, or use store-bought cutlets)
- 1 teaspoon salt
- ½ cup all-purpose flour
- 4 tablespoons olive oil, plus more as needed

COOK'S NOTE

If at any point you reheat the chutney, consider stirring in a couple of additional tablespoons of cider vinegar.

Simple Chicken Scaloppine
with Quick Prune Chutney

Many think of scaloppine as a specific Italian dish served with a lemon-caper sauce, but it actually refers to a general preparation of thinly sliced meat dredged in flour, panfried, and served with any reduced sauce.

While a bit unconventional, here we have cutlets that have been dredged in flour and panfried — so far, so good — and topped with chutney. My quick chutney is a sauce of prunes cooked down (reduced!) with vinegar and some sugar, which I say counts as part of the definition.

So there you go. Scaloppine.

1 **MAKE THE CHUTNEY:** Melt the butter in a small saucepan set over medium heat. Add the shallots and sauté until softened, 3 minutes. Add the prunes, toss to coat well, and sauté for 1 minute. Add the sugar and mustard; stir to combine and cook for 2 minutes. Add the vinegar, ¼ cup of water, the salt, and the cinnamon. Reduce the heat to low and very gently simmer until the mixture slightly thickens to the desired consistency, 6 to 7 minutes. Remove from the heat and set aside.

2 **MAKE THE CHICKEN:** Pat the chicken dry with paper towels and season with the salt, evenly dividing it between both sides of all the cutlets. Add the flour to a medium, shallow bowl and dredge the cutlets in the flour, shaking off the excess before setting the cutlets aside.

3 Warm the oil in a large heavy skillet set over medium-high heat. Once the oil is hot, add the cutlets in a single layer and sauté until cooked through, 6 to 7 minutes, flipping halfway through the cooking time.

If you have to cook your cutlets in batches, note that you may have to add an extra drizzle of oil and slightly reduce the heat to prevent burning, which may impact cooking time for the second batch.

4 Serve the cutlets right away with chutney spooned over the top.

Five-Spice Cutlets
with Asian Cabbage Slaw

4 servings

INGREDIENTS

FOR THE CHICKEN

- 1½ tablespoons five-spice powder
- 2 teaspoons salt
- 1 teaspoon freshly ground black pepper
- 2 pounds boneless, skinless chicken breasts, butterflied (page 36, or use store-bought cutlets)
- 3 tablespoons neutral oil, such as grapeseed, plus more as needed

FOR THE SLAW

- 1 garlic clove, finely minced or grated
- ¼ cup unseasoned rice wine vinegar
- ¼ cup neutral oil, such as grapeseed
- 2 tablespoons soy sauce
- 2 tablespoons lime juice (from about 1 juicy lime)
- 1 tablespoon toasted sesame oil
- 3 cups shredded cabbage (I like using a combination of green or napa and purple cabbage)
- 5 thinly sliced scallions, light and dark green parts only
- 1 cup shredded carrots
- 1 cup thinly sliced snap peas, cut lengthwise or julienne
- Chopped fresh cilantro, to taste (optional)

It seemed strange to write a cookbook on chicken without including a recipe for paillard, a French preparation of a thin piece of meat that has been pounded flat and quickly grilled or sautéed. This recipe was meant to be my fun twist on paillard, but I decided that there was no good reason to spend time pounding cutlets for a dinner this quick and casual.

The thing is, no pounding means this recipe is technically not paillard. So Five-Spice Cutlets they are. I can live with that.

If five-spice isn't your jam, go with another spice blend and make a different kind of quick slaw, relish, or salsa.

1 **MAKE THE CHICKEN:** In a small bowl, combine the five-spice powder, salt, and pepper. Pat the chicken dry with paper towels and sprinkle with the spice mixture, evenly dividing it between both sides of all the cutlets.

2 Warm the oil in a large heavy skillet set over medium-high heat. Once the oil is hot, add the cutlets in a single layer and sauté until cooked through, 6 to 7 minutes, flipping halfway through the cooking time. Transfer the cutlets to a plate. Once they've rested for about 5 minutes, season to taste with more salt, if desired.

If you have to cook your cutlets in batches, note that you may have to add an extra drizzle of oil and slightly reduce the heat to prevent burning, which may impact cooking time for the second batch.

3 **MAKE THE SLAW:** Add the garlic to a jar with a tightly fitted lid and cover it with the vinegar. If you have time, allow it to sit for a few minutes to mellow. (I like to assemble the veggies at this point.) Add the neutral oil, soy sauce, lime juice, and sesame oil. Seal the jar and shake well.

Add the cabbage, scallions, carrots, snap peas, and cilantro to a large bowl and toss well with the dressing. Serve alongside or over the top of the cutlets.

INGREDIENTS

5 tablespoons low-sodium soy sauce

4 tablespoons unseasoned rice wine vinegar

2 tablespoons chicken stock (homemade, page 99, or store-bought)

1 tablespoon cornstarch

4 tablespoons neutral oil, such as grapeseed, plus more as needed

1½ pounds boneless, skinless chicken breasts or chicken thighs, cut into 2-inch pieces

½ teaspoon salt

12 ounces green beans, trimmed and cut in half

2 bell peppers, cut into ½-inch-thick strips (I like using 1 red and 1 yellow or orange pepper)

5 garlic cloves, finely minced or grated

¼ teaspoon red pepper flakes

2 cups (about 2 ounces) basil leaves (Thai basil if you can find it)

Cooked rice, for serving (optional)

Basil Chicken and Vegetable Stir-Fry

This is my favorite weeknight stir-fry (which, far be it from me to say the b-word, is also delicious made with beef). The key to making this — and really, *any* stir-fry — successfully is to work quickly with high heat. And that means being prepared.

More than with any other recipe in this book, please, please, please: prep everything ahead of time and keep your *mise en place* (fancy for *prepped ingredients*) within an arm's reach by the stove. And no multitasking. Then get your skillet or wok searing hot and go!

Getting your timing off by even a little bit can mean overcooked chicken, burnt veggies, and/or not enough sauce — all of which are a bummer, even if the overall flavor is spot on.

1 Whisk together the soy sauce, vinegar, stock, and cornstarch in a small bowl or medium measuring cup; set aside, keeping the whisk close by.

2 Place a large skillet or wok over high heat for 30 seconds. Add 2 tablespoons of the oil and heat until shimmering, about 30 seconds. Add the chicken and sprinkle with ¼ teaspoon of the salt. Cook, tossing frequently, until browned on all sides, about 5 minutes. Transfer the chicken to a plate.

3 Add the remaining 2 tablespoons oil to the skillet or wok and as soon as the oil is shimmering — which may very well be immediately — add the green beans and bell peppers. Sprinkle with the remaining ¼ teaspoon salt and cook, tossing frequently, until just tender and charred in spots, about 4 minutes.

If at any point in this or subsequent steps the oil cooks off or the mixture begins to burn, reduce the heat to medium-high (but not lower). You can also add a small additional glug of oil.

4 Push the vegetables to the edges of the skillet or wok and add the garlic and pepper flakes to the open space in the middle. Cook, keeping them contained in the center space, but moving them around to prevent burning, for about 20 seconds.

5 Return the chicken and any accumulated juices to the skillet or wok and toss everything together once. Give your stir-fry sauce a whisk (the cornstarch likely settled to the bottom) and add it to the skillet or wok. Cook, tossing constantly, until the sauce thickens and coats all of the ingredients, 30 to 60 seconds. Remove from the heat, add the basil, and serve immediately, over rice, if desired.

Chicken with 40 Cloves of Garlic

4 servings

INGREDIENTS

- 8 bone-in, skin-on chicken thighs (3 to 4 pounds)
- 1 teaspoon salt
- 1 teaspoon freshly ground black pepper
- 3 tablespoons unsalted butter, plus 2 tablespoons softened
- 40 garlic cloves, peeled and trimmed (from 2 extra-large or 3 heads of garlic)
- 1 cup white wine
- ¼ cup chicken stock (homemade, page 99, or store-bought)
- 5 sprigs fresh thyme
- 2 tablespoons all-purpose flour

COOK'S NOTE

If you have the time to dry brine, you won't regret it. Follow the directions on page 51 and skip the salt in this recipe.

Don't be scared: your breath will not be kicking after you eat this dish.

Or maybe you want it to be? This is not the meal to make when you're trying to have the breakup conversation (for that, see Lebanese Garlic Sauce, page 60). This classic French dish with wine, butter, fresh thyme, and tons of mellowed-out garlic will only make someone fall deeper in love with you.

Because of course the French know that done right, garlic is a love language.

1 If you have time, remove the chicken from your refrigerator up to 30 minutes before cooking. When ready to cook, pat the chicken dry with paper towels and season it with the salt and pepper, evenly dividing them between both sides of all the thighs.

Heat 3 tablespoons of the butter in a large heavy sauté pan set over medium-high heat and add the chicken, skin side down. Cook until browned, 5 to 7 minutes, then flip and cook until browned on the other side, about 3 minutes longer. Transfer the chicken to a plate.

2 Reduce the heat to medium and add the garlic to the pan. Sauté, stirring frequently, until browned on all sides, about 4 minutes. Add the wine, stock, and thyme, scraping up the crispy bits. Return the chicken skin side up to the pan, along with accumulated juices, lower the heat to medium-low (or whatever gets you to a gentle simmer), cover, and cook until the chicken cooks through, 10 to 12 minutes; an instant-read thermometer should register 165°F (75°C) at the thickest part of the thigh. If the chicken isn't cooked through, cook for a few minutes longer until it is. Turn off the heat and transfer the chicken to a plate.

3 Using a fork, mash together the 2 tablespoons softened butter and the flour in a medium bowl to make a paste. Ladle some of the hot sauce from the pan into the bowl and slowly whisk it with the paste until smooth. Turn the heat back on to medium and add the butter-flour mixture to the pan. Bring it to a gentle boil, whisking constantly, and cook until the sauce thickens, about 1 minute. Season to taste with more salt and pepper, if desired. Return the chicken skin side up to the pan, along with any accumulated juices, and serve immediately.

Chicken with Mushrooms
in a Sherry Cream Sauce

4 servings

INGREDIENTS

- 2 pounds boneless, skinless chicken breasts, butterflied (page 36, or use store-bought cutlets)
- 1¾ teaspoons salt
- 1 teaspoon freshly ground black pepper
- 3 tablespoons olive oil, plus more as needed
- 1 pound cremini (a.k.a. baby bella) mushrooms, wiped clean, trimmed, and sliced
- 5 garlic cloves, finely chopped
- ½ cup dry sherry or port
- 2 tablespoons unsalted butter
- 1½ cups heavy cream
- ⅓ cup grated Parmesan cheese, plus more for serving (you can substitute Grana Padano, page 94)
- Cooked pasta, for serving (optional)
- Fresh parsley, for garnish (optional)

I usually serve this dish over pasta — because what could be better? When I'm in a major rush, though, or I already have rice or pretty much any other carb on hand, I skip the pasta and simply smother the chicken in saucy goodness.

You can make this with white wine, too, but if you do that and enjoy this enough to make it again, use sherry or port. They boost the flavor like you wouldn't believe.

1 Pat the chicken dry with paper towels and season with 1½ teaspoons of the salt and the pepper, evenly dividing them between both sides of all the chicken breasts; set aside.

2 Warm the oil in a large heavy sauté pan set over medium-high heat. Once the oil is hot, add the cutlets in a single layer and cook until cooked through, 6 to 7 minutes, flipping halfway through the cooking time. Transfer the cutlets to a plate.

If you have to cook your cutlets in batches, note that you may have to add an extra drizzle of oil and slightly reduce the heat to prevent burning, which may impact cooking time for the second batch.

3 Reduce the heat to medium. Add the mushrooms, garlic, and the remaining ¼ teaspoon salt to the pan. Toss to coat, 20 to 30 seconds, then add the sherry. Cook, using a wooden spoon or silicone spatula to scrape up the crispy bits, until the sherry is nearly gone, 6 to 7 minutes. Add the butter and swirl to coat the mushrooms well.

4 Once the butter melts completely, add the cream and stir to combine. Return the chicken to the pan, along with any accumulated juices, and bring just to a boil. Reduce the heat to medium-low (or whatever you need to get a gentle simmer) and cook until the sauce thickens slightly, about 3 minutes.

Remove the pan from the heat and stir the Parmesan into the sauce. Serve over pasta, if desired, topped with extra cheese and the parsley, if using.

Chicken Paprikash

INGREDIENTS

- 4 bone-in, skin-on chicken leg quarters, split
- ¾ cup sour cream
- 1½ teaspoons salt
- 1 teaspoon freshly ground black pepper
- 1 tablespoon neutral oil, such as grapeseed
- 1 tablespoon unsalted butter
- 1 large onion, thinly sliced
- 3 large garlic cloves, finely minced or grated
- 3 tablespoons sweet Hungarian paprika or a combination of sweet and hot paprika (see page 90)
- 3 cups chicken stock (homemade, page 99, or store-bought)
- 1½ teaspoons lemon juice (from about ¼ a juicy lemon)
- Fresh parsley, for garnish (optional)
- Buttered egg noodles, for serving

I can't explain why I love chicken paprikash so much given my Greek heritage, but I do. In fact, a simpler version made with easy-to-cut chicken breast that I made for my oldest son when he was just a toddler was one of my first food blog posts.

Now — *many* years later — he loves it, too, but he's got some Hungarian blood, so I guess he comes by it more honestly. If you serve this over buttered egg noodles (a comfort food in its own right), I think you'll fall in love with chicken paprikash, too.

1 If you have time, remove the chicken from your refrigerator up to 1 hour before cooking. Also take the sour cream out of the refrigerator as soon as possible to come to room temperature. When ready to cook, pat the chicken dry with paper towels and season it with 1 teaspoon of the salt and the pepper, evenly dividing them between both sides of all the chicken pieces.

Heat the oil and butter in a large sauté pan set over medium-high heat. Once the butter begins to foam, add the chicken skin side down, making sure to press it as flat as possible onto the hot surface, and cook for 7 to 8 minutes. Flip and cook the other side for 7 to 8 minutes longer. Transfer the chicken to a plate.

2 Reduce the heat to medium and add the onion. Cook for 3 minutes and, using a wooden spoon or silicone spatula, stir occasionally to scrape up the crispy bits as you go. Add the garlic and cook for 3 minutes longer. Add the paprika and, stirring constantly to prevent it from burning, cook for 1 minute.

3 Add the stock and the remaining ½ teaspoon salt, and stir to incorporate. Return the chicken to the pan along with any accumulated juices and adjust the heat to bring to a simmer. Cook until the chicken is cooked through, 12 to 15 minutes; an instant-read thermometer should register 165°F (75°C) at the thickest part of the leg and thigh.

Note: If you want to maintain crispy skin, be sure to return the chicken to the pan skin side up and leave it that way for the entire 12 to 15 minutes. If you'd rather have stewed-style chicken, flip the chicken halfway through the cooking time; you can pull the skin off before serving.

Transfer the chicken to a plate.

4 Place the room-temperature sour cream in a medium bowl and carefully spoon small amounts of the hot sauce from the pan into the sour cream to temper it, mixing each spoonful in before adding the next. Once you've added enough hot sauce to make the sour cream very warm to the touch, add all of it to the sauté pan and stir well to incorporate.

Add the lemon juice and season to taste with more lemon juice, salt, and pepper, if needed. Return the chicken to the sauté pan and garnish with parsley, if desired, before serving immediately on top of buttered egg noodles.

COOK'S NOTES

Split leg quarters are usually sold at supermarkets as "chicken drumsticks and thighs," with one package containing two drumsticks and two thighs. Alternatively, you may have to buy the bone-in, skin-on drumsticks and thighs separately, or you can buy whole leg quarters (the drumsticks and thighs still connected) and split them in half yourself (see page 28). You need four drumsticks and four thighs, total, for this recipe.

If you have the time to dry brine, you won't regret it. Follow the directions on page 51 and skip the salt in this recipe.

ALL ABOUT PAPRIKA: SOME LIKE IT HOT

Not all paprika is created equal. While you can easily use the generic paprika available in your local supermarket, paprikash (page 88) is much better made with the real-deal Hungarian stuff, which has a deeper, more intense flavor. And in general, quality matters, especially for dishes where paprika is the star.

Freshness matters, too. In fact, if your supermarket paprika has been hanging around your spice cabinet for a few years, do yourself a favor and get a new stash. I recommend buying paprika — and spices, in general — in smaller quantities that you can use up while still fresh. This also allows you to play around: maybe buy both sweet and hot paprika.

If want a little heat in your paprikash, use a combination of sweet and hot Hungarian paprika or, if it's easier, add a little cayenne *in addition* to the sweet paprika called for in a recipe. Just keep in mind that even ¼ teaspoon of cayenne goes a long way to spice things up.

Arroz con Pollo

4 servings

INGREDIENTS

- 4 bone-in, skin-on chicken leg quarters, split (see note, page 92)
- 1½ teaspoons salt
- 1 teaspoon freshly ground black pepper
- 2 tablespoons olive oil
- 6 large garlic cloves, finely minced or grated
- 1 red bell pepper, chopped
- 1 green bell pepper, chopped
- 1 onion, chopped
- 1 tablespoon dried oregano
- 1 tablespoon ground cumin
- 2 teaspoons garlic powder
- 1½ teaspoons ground coriander
- 1 teaspoon smoked paprika
- 1 cup lager beer (you can substitute 1 cup chicken stock)
- 1 cup chicken stock (homemade, page 99, or store-bought)
- 1 cup canned chopped tomatoes
- 1 cup long-grain white rice
- 1 cup frozen green peas
- 1 cup chopped green olive salad with pimentos (you can substitute chopped green olives)
- 3 tablespoons red wine vinegar
- Fresh cilantro, for garnish (optional)

New York City has a very large Puerto Rican population thanks to its proximity to that beautiful island, which I've been lucky enough to visit four times, and lots of great Puerto Rican food. In an effort to get to know Puerto Rican cooking better, I spent the better part of one year cooking it frequently, culminating my self-study with a Puerto Rican Christmas dinner, a big surprise for my Greek family. (Everyone loved it!)

Though it's a bit cliché, one of my family's favorite Puerto Rican dishes is arroz con pollo, a popular dish made with variations throughout the Caribbean. The Puerto Rican version is often made with beer, which I use here, and annatto seed, which I left out because it can be hard to find. If you spy it, though, grab some and look up how to make annatto oil, then use it in place of the olive oil here. It's worth it.

1 If you have time, remove the chicken from your refrigerator up to 1 hour before cooking. When ready to cook, pat the chicken dry with paper towels and season with 1 teaspoon of the salt and the black pepper, evenly dividing them among all of the chicken pieces on both sides.

Heat the oil in a large sauté pan set over medium-high heat. Add the chicken skin side down, making sure to press it as flat as possible onto the hot surface, and cook for 7 to 8 minutes. Flip and cook the other side for an additional 7 to 8 minutes. Transfer the chicken to a plate.

2 Lower the heat to medium-low and sauté the garlic, red and green bell peppers, and onion until fragrant, about 3 minutes. Add the oregano, cumin, garlic powder, coriander, and paprika, and cook, stirring constantly to keep the spices from burning, another 2 minutes.

3 Add the beer and cook for 1 minute, using a wooden spoon or silicone spatula to scrape up the crispy bits. Add the stock and tomatoes. Raise the heat to medium and bring to just barely a simmer, about 1½ minutes, then add the rice, stirring to evenly distribute. Return the chicken to the pan skin side up in a single layer, along with any accumulated juices, return the heat to medium-low, cover, and very lightly simmer until the rice and chicken are cooked through, about 30 minutes.

Turn off the heat, uncover, and quickly add the remaining ½ teaspoon salt, the peas, and olives. Cover again and allow the pan to sit for another 5 minutes.

4 Uncover, drizzle with vinegar, and season to taste with more salt and black pepper as desired. Serve with cilantro over the top, if desired.

COOK'S NOTES

Split leg quarters are usually sold at supermarkets as "chicken drumsticks and thighs," with one package containing two drumsticks and two thighs. Alternatively, you may have to buy the bone-in, skin-on drumsticks and thighs separately, or you can buy whole leg quarters (the drumsticks and thighs still connected) and split them in half yourself (see page 28). You need four drumsticks and four thighs, total, for Arroz con Pollo.

If you have the time to dry brine, you won't regret it. Follow the directions on page 51 and skip the salt in the recipe.

ANY KIND OF ARROZ WITH ANY KIND OF POLLO

While my arroz con pollo has a decidedly Latin flare — it's inspired by a Puerto Rican version — you can use the recipe on page 91 as a template to make all manner of chicken and rice in one sauté pan. Here's how:

START BY BROWNING BONE-IN, SKIN-ON PIECES; you can use a whole cut-up bird, all legs, all thighs, or whatever you fancy. Once they've browned for 7 to 8 minutes per side, allow them to rest while you work on the next step.

SAUTÉ GARLIC AND/OR ONION, along with any (nonfrozen) chopped vegetables for 3 to 5 minutes. Add spices and aromatics next, and sauté for about 2 minutes.

ADD 1 CUP CHOPPED TOMATOES AND 2 CUPS OF COOKING LIQUID, which can be wine, stock, water, or any combination thereof. When finished, garnish with whatever ingredients match the flavor profile you're working with. For example, here's how you'd make chicken and rice with an Indian flair:

Sauté onion, garlic, and cut-up green beans — perhaps in coconut oil or ghee instead of olive oil. For spice, toast a teaspoon each of cumin, coriander, turmeric, and freshly grated ginger. Then add the chopped tomatoes and a combination of white wine and stock. When you add the rice, you can also add a whole cardamom pod and/or a star anise seed. Finish with frozen peas or a combination of frozen peas and carrots, and serve garnished with cilantro, plain yogurt, and toasted almonds.

COOK'S NOTE

You don't have to spend all of your hard-earned cash on pricey imported Parmesan, thanks to Grana Padano. If you're unfamiliar with this hard Italian cheese, it's quite similar to Parmesan, with a sharp, nutty flavor. Though milder than Parmesan, the two are pretty much interchangeable in the home kitchen. Plus, Grana Padano comes at a much more affordable price. When looking to buy Grana Padano, just like with Parmesan, keep your eyes peeled for the real deal imported from Italy.

Chicken Parmesan Meatballs

4 servings

INGREDIENTS

- 1½ pounds ground chicken, preferably dark meat
- 3 garlic cloves, finely minced or grated
- ¾ cup grated Parmesan cheese (you can substitute Grana Padano; see note on page 94)
- ½ cup plain Italian-style breadcrumbs
- 3 tablespoons tomato paste
- 1 egg, lightly beaten
- 1½ teaspoons dried oregano
- 1¼ teaspoons freshly ground black pepper
- 1 teaspoon salt
- ½ teaspoon onion powder
- 4 ounces low-moisture mozzarella cheese, cut into ½-inch chunks
- 3 tablespoons olive oil, plus more as needed
- 2½ cups favorite marinara sauce
- Fresh basil, torn into pieces, for garnish (optional)
- Garlic bread, for serving (optional)

When introducing my Caprese Sheet Pan Chicken (page 71), I mentioned wanting to come up with a playful way to include Chicken Parmesan in this book, and if you ask me, nothing is more fun than meatballs. You can serve them small, medium, or giant; as dinner or an appetizer; over pasta, with bread, in a sandwich, or just in a baking dish with sauce and melty cheese on top. The possibilities are endless, and we haven't even gotten to the millions of ways that you can flavor meatballs.

Why would we do that when we've got the best version right here?

I stuff these with mozzarella and garnish with grated Parmesan. But I have a confession: I've also made these with even more mozzarella melted on top. If you want to do that, too, you'll need more mozzarella than called for in the recipe. And, yes, it's worth it.

1 Place the chicken, garlic, ½ cup of the Parmesan, the breadcrumbs, tomato paste, egg, oregano, pepper, salt, and onion powder in a large mixing bowl and, using your hands, a wooden spoon, or a silicone spatula, combine well, being careful not to overmix.

2 Lightly wet your hands before rolling the meat mixture into golf ball–size meatballs (about 1½ inches), each stuffed with a small piece of mozzarella in the middle.

3 Heat the oil in a large heavy sauté pan set over medium heat. Add the meatballs, being careful not to overcrowd (you may have to do this in batches). Fry until browned, turning the meatballs two or three times so that they brown all around, 6 to 8 minutes.

If you do cook the meatballs in batches, note that you may have to add an extra drizzle of oil, especially if using white meat.

4 Once all of the meatballs have browned, cover them with sauce in the pan. Keep at medium heat or adjust to whatever you need to bring the sauce to a simmer, cover, and cook until the largest of the meatballs are cooked through, 5 to 8 minutes, depending on the size of the meatballs.

5 Sprinkle the meatballs with the remaining ¼ cup Parmesan and the torn basil leaves, if using. Season to taste with more salt as desired. Serve with thick-cut garlic bread, if desired.

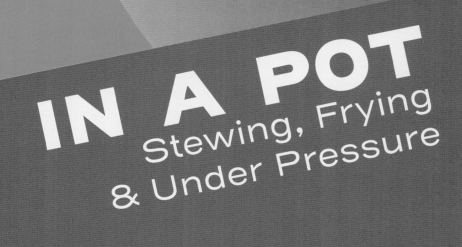

IN A POT
Stewing, Frying
& Under Pressure

When you pull out a pot — whether a stockpot, Dutch oven, or the insert of an electric pressure cooker — chances are a comfort meal is coming. When it comes to chicken, my favorite comfort meals are soups, chili, stews, and curries. And fast food–style fried chicken, too, because that's what I grew up eating (every Tuesday on the way home from Greek school!).

I decided to include electric pressure cooker recipes because they help make many comfort food dishes more realistic, especially during the week. A recipe that normally slow cooks on the stove for a couple of hours can go from prep to table in 30 minutes or less using one. That's a major boon for busy home cooks.

Since I'd love for all of the recipes in this chapter to work for people who don't own an electric pressure cooker, I added notes on turning those recipes into ones that you can make on the stove, too. Just keep in mind that adjustments may be needed since the lids of electric pressure cookers seal tightly, allowing for little to no evaporation.

Converting recipes this way isn't an exact science, but between my notes and your senses — watch, smell, and taste as you go — these recipes are forgiving enough that you will be fine!

STOCK VERSUS BROTH

THOUGH STOCK AND BROTH are often used interchangeably, they are two different things. Typically, stock is made with raw, meaty bones. By meaty, I mean ones that may still have a little bit of flesh on them, like the backbone and wings left over after breaking down a whole chicken (page 25). Or if you get bone-in, skin-on chicken breasts and take the meat off of the bones yourself, they are likely to be a little meaty. All good for stock!

In my recipe for Chicken Stock (page 99) I describe using a combination of raw bones and the bones left over from a cooked bird in a pinch. This is technically a cheat, but it works. And hey, you're not in culinary school. (Or are you?)

There's not much more to say about broth other than it's made with a whole bird or chicken pieces with all the meat still on the bone. An example of broth is my Quick Chicken Soup (page 103).

Freezing Stock

One of the many virtues of homemade stock (or broth) is that it freezes beautifully. You can make it whenever you have the ingredients and time, and then store it in the freezer (for up to three months) for when you need it next.

Make sure that your broth has cooled completely, and skim the fat before you pack it up for the freezer. Many sources suggest freezing stock in ice cube trays. While this can be space efficient — which is not a small deal — I find that the small amounts are a bit inconvenient. I prefer to store my broth in plastic or reusable silicone food storage bags in 1-cup amounts. When frozen while laid flat, bags with this amount of stock can be space efficient, too.

Boosting Store-Bought Stock or Broth

Making homemade stock isn't always an option, which is why I keep store-bought on hand. But even the best commercial brands don't quite measure up. If you need to use store-bought in a recipe, especially one where the flavor is going to be front and center, consider giving it a boost by simmering it with fresh ingredients to brighten the flavor.

Simmer every 32-ounce box of stock or broth for 15 to 20 minutes with one large carrot and two stalks of celery (each cut into three pieces); a small onion peeled, trimmed at the root, and cut into quarters; and a few sprigs of fresh parsley or the tops of the celery. You can throw in a few sprigs of thyme, too, if you want. When done, strain the stock or broth and discard the solids before using as desired.

Chicken Stock

Makes 8 cups (2 quarts)

INGREDIENTS

- 4 pounds raw chicken bones
- 2 stalks celery, each roughly cut into 3 pieces
- 1 large onion, halved lengthwise, trimmed at the root, and peeled
- 1 large carrot, roughly cut into 3 pieces
- 2 teaspoons salt
- 10 whole black peppercorns
- 10 sprigs parsley
- 1 bay leaf

Every cook should know how to make this basic recipe. It usually takes two carcasses to get four pounds of bones. If you want to be a real chicken ninja — and also save tons of money — buy two whole birds, take 30 minutes or so to break them down, pack the cuts up between the fridge (for the week) and the freezer (for later use), and make stock.

Another option is to ask a butcher for four pounds of bones to throw straight into a stockpot or, if you plan on buying one bird to break down on your own, ask the butcher to supplement with two pounds of bones.

Before using stock in a recipe, be sure to skim the fat from the top. The easiest way to do this is to refrigerate the stock and scoop the congealed fat right off the top. If you don't have time for that, a gravy separator will do the job.

1 Add the chicken bones to a large stockpot along with the celery, onion, carrot, salt, peppercorns, parsley, and bay leaf. Cover with 5 quarts of warm water, or enough water to cover the bones by about 2 inches. Set the pot over high heat and bring just to a boil.

2 Reduce to a simmer and cook for 4 to 5 hours, periodically skimming the surface of any fat and foam. If the water evaporates too quickly, don't be shy about adding more, especially if you plan to simmer this for the full 5 hours, which is ideal for maximum flavor.

3 Allow the broth to cool completely, for several hours, before straining. Be sure to press down on the veggies to extract any broth that they've absorbed before discarding them. Store the broth in the refrigerator for up to 5 days and in the freezer for up to 3 months.

COOK'S NOTES

You can use a combination of raw bones and what's left from a cooked chicken to make this stock, so don't throw away that roast chicken carcass! While technically a departure from classic stock, which is made entirely from raw bones, I find this a practical approach since home cooks don't often find themselves with four pounds of raw chicken bones on their hands unless they expressly set out to make chicken stock.

This stock is low in sodium so that it can be used in any recipe without interfering with the flavor or saltiness of the dish. If you end up using it for soup, stew, or any dish for which it will be the primary ingredient, keep in mind that you'll likely have to add a generous amount of salt to taste.

Classic Brown Chicken Stock

Makes 8 cups (2 quarts)

INGREDIENTS

- Neutral oil, such as grapeseed
- 4 pounds raw chicken bones
- 2 stalks celery, each roughly cut into 3 pieces
- 1 large onion, halved lengthwise, trimmed at the root, and peeled
- 1 large carrot, roughly cut into 3 pieces
- 1 tablespoon tomato paste
- White wine or water
- 2 teaspoons salt
- 10 whole black peppercorns
- 10 sprigs parsley, just the stems, washed
- 5 sprigs fresh thyme
- 1 bay leaf

Regular chicken stock gives you a clean, crisp, light color and flavor, but when you want a stock with richer taste — one great for hearty stews, boldly flavored soups, and any recipe, especially a sauce, with a deep umami flavor — this is the one to use.

This stock is low in sodium so that it can be used in any recipe without interfering with the flavor or saltiness of the dish. If you end up using this for soup, stew, or any dish for which this will be the primary ingredient, keep in mind that you'll likely have to add a generous amount of salt to taste.

1 Preheat the oven to 425°F (220°C) and very lightly oil a large sheet pan. Place the chicken bones on the sheet and roast for about 45 minutes, until dark golden brown, being careful not to burn the bones, which can cause a bitter flavor.

2 While the bones cook, lightly oil another large sheet pan. Add the celery, onion, and carrot, and roast for 30 minutes. After 10 minutes, remove the vegetables from the oven and carefully toss them with the tomato paste before returning them to the oven for the remaining 20 minutes.

Note: If you start cooking the vegetables 15 minutes after the bones go into the oven, everything will be done at the same time.

3 Once the bones and vegetables are done roasting, add everything from both baking sheets to a stockpot. Include any rendered chicken fat.

4 Place the baking sheet that had the bones on it onto your stovetop over medium heat (it will straddle two burners). Add a few hearty glugs of white wine or water and, using a wooden spoon or silicone spatula, scrape up the crispy bits. As soon as you get all of them up off of the pan, turn off the burners and toss the cooking liquid with all the scraped-up bits into the stockpot, too.

5 Add the salt, peppercorns, parsley, thyme, and bay leaf to the stockpot, along with 5 quarts of warm water, or enough water to cover the bones by about 2 inches. Set the pot over high heat and bring just to a boil.

6 Reduce to a simmer and cook for 4 to 5 hours, periodically skimming the surface of any fat and foam. If the water evaporates too quickly, don't be shy about adding more, especially if you plan to simmer this for the full 5 hours, which is ideal for maximum flavor.

7 Allow the stock to cool completely, for several hours, before straining. Be sure to press down on the veggies to extract any stock that they've absorbed before discarding them. Store the stock in the refrigerator for up to 5 days and in the freezer for up to 3 months.

COOK'S NOTE

Classic brown stock is made by roasting raw bones that have been stripped of most of their meat, which is different than using the leftover bones of a roasted chicken. Though a roasted chicken carcass has been in the oven, those bones were roasted while completely covered with muscle tissue and skin, which essentially caused them to steam. A stock made with bones cooked that way will give you a much cleaner flavor that makes more sense for a classic stock recipe (hence my Cook's Notes on page 99).

If you want to make a brown stock using the carcass from a leftover roasted chicken (or turkey), re-roast them once they are stripped of meat using the method given here. The result won't be quite the same, but the flavor will be much more full bodied than if you just threw the leftover carcass into a pot with water, veggies, and aromatics.

OTHER SOUP ADD-INS

- Add 1 large carrot and 2 stalks celery, both cut into a ¼-inch dice, to the simmering broth after you remove the bay leaf and peppercorns, and cook for 12 to 15 minutes, or until tender.

- Add 2 cups of egg noodles to the simmering broth after you remove the bay leaf and peppercorns, and cook for 10 minutes.

- Add ½ cup of pastina or orzo to the simmering broth after you remove the bay leaf and peppercorns, and cook for 5 to 8 minutes.

- Add 1 cup of long-grain white rice to the simmering broth after you remove the bay leaf and peppercorns. Partially cover the pot, lower the heat, and cook until the rice is cooked through, about 18 minutes.

Quick Chicken Soup

4–6 servings

INGREDIENTS

1 whole, bone-in, skin-on chicken breast, split

1 teaspoon salt

2 tablespoons olive oil

1 large onion, chopped

10 whole black peppercorns

1 bay leaf

Freshly ground black pepper (optional)

The traditional way to make chicken soup is to start by making a stock (see pages 99–101) that becomes the base to which you add everything else. If you're making a Greek-style avgolemono, you'll add rice, whisked eggs, and lemon juice. If you're making egg drop soup, you'll add soy sauce, a cornstarch slurry, and whisked eggs. If you're making matzoh ball soup, you'll add carrots and, of course, matzoh balls. And so on.

But when I want a superquick chicken soup chock-full of meat, I use this method that I discovered years ago, I believe from *Cook's Illustrated*. Once I discovered it, the days of wrestling a whole bird into a huge stockpot, covering it completely with water, and waiting for hours the way that my grandmother did were instantly a thing of my past. Now a regular pot and just about 30 minutes do the job.

1 Set a medium pot filled with 8 cups of water over medium heat to boil. (If the water comes to a boil before you're ready to use it, reduce the heat to keep it very hot, but not boiling so that you don't lose volume.) In the meantime, season the chicken with ½ teaspoon of the salt, dividing it equally between both sides of both breast halves. Heat the oil in a large pot set over medium heat and add the chicken breast halves, skin side down. Cook for about 12 minutes, flipping the chicken halfway through. Transfer the chicken to a plate.

2 Add the onion to the large pot and sauté until translucent, using a wooden spoon or silicone spatula to scrape up the crispy bits, about 3 minutes.

3 Return the chicken to the large pot, along with any accumulated juices, and add the peppercorns and bay leaf. Pour the hot water over the chicken. Return to a boil, reduce the heat to medium-low, cover, and very gently simmer for 25 minutes.

4 Turn off the heat and remove the chicken from the broth to cool. Using a slotted spoon, remove the bay leaf and peppercorns. It's okay to get rid of some of the onions, too, though I like leaving a few. Season the broth with the remaining ½ teaspoon salt, adding more to taste, along with ground black pepper if you wish.

5 Once the chicken is cool enough to handle, remove the skin and pull the meat from the bone. Add all or some of the meat to the broth, if desired. If serving immediately, season to taste with even more salt and pepper as desired. Otherwise, allow the soup to cool completely before sealing and storing in the refrigerator for up to 5 days.

If storing any chicken separately from the broth, add it to a container and spoon some broth on top to help keep it moist; allow both to cool completely before sealing and storing in the refrigerator for up to 5 days.

Chicken Laarb

4 servings

INGREDIENTS

- ¼ cup chicken stock
- 3 garlic cloves, finely minced or grated
- ½ teaspoon salt
- ½ teaspoon dark brown or light brown sugar
- 1½ pounds ground dark meat chicken
- 4–5 tablespoons lime juice (from 2 to 3 juicy limes)
- 2 tablespoons fish sauce
- 3 shallots, halved, peeled, and very thinly sliced
- ¼ cup chopped fresh cilantro
- ¼ cup chopped fresh mint
- 1 Thai chile, thinly sliced (optional; you can also substitute Sriracha to taste)

COOK'S NOTE

Laarb is traditionally finished with a toasted rice powder that gives it a great finish and texture. It's worth the extra time if you'd like to add some:

Add 2 tablespoons of jasmine or long-grain rice to a small skillet set over medium heat and cook, shaking frequently, until golden brown, 8 to 10 minutes. Transfer the toasted rice to a mini-chop, food processor, or high-powered blender and process into a fine powder. Stir into the laarb right before serving.

I fell in love with laarb (also known as larb or larp) — a minced meat salad usually made of chicken or pork — years ago on a trip through Southeast Asia. I've usually had it served at room temperature with sticky rice and veggies like cold sliced cucumber, but you can serve it warm or cold. Many like serving it in lettuce cups, which makes a nice summer dinner with a big pot of rice.

A lot of recipes for laarb call for lemongrass and kaffir lime leaf. Not only are both hard to find, but in Thailand I learned a simpler version made with a dressing of just lime juice and fish sauce.

Traditionally, a spicy Thai chili powder gives this dish its sour, salty heat. I opt for fresh chiles instead, so that you can more easily control the heat. But by all means, if you like spicy, look for Thai chili powder and experiment.

1. Combine the stock, garlic, salt, and sugar in a medium pot set over medium heat and cook until the salt and sugar dissolve, about 2 minutes.

2. Add the chicken and cook until it is cooked through, about 8 minutes. In that time, use a wooden spoon or silicone spatula to gently break up the meat just three or four times, but otherwise leave it alone. You want to be careful not to mess with it too much during this step or it will get tough. Using a slotted spoon, transfer the cooked chicken to a large serving bowl and allow it to come to room temperature. Discard the cooking liquid.

3. To make the dressing, whisk 4 tablespoons of the lime juice with the fish sauce. (If using Sriracha instead of the fresh chile, add that, too.)

4. Add the shallots, cilantro, mint, and chile, if using, to the chicken. Toss with three-fourths of the dressing to coat everything well.

Adjust the seasoning to taste: it should be booming with flavor and balanced between sour and salty. If you need more sour, add the remaining 1 tablespoon lime juice. If you need more salt, add fish sauce in very small amounts, tasting as you go, until it's just right.

You can also add more heat by throwing in more chiles (or Sriracha). Serve immediately or store in the refrigerator for up to 3 days to reheat or serve cold.

Chicken Thigh Ragu

INGREDIENTS

- 1 (28-ounce) can whole peeled tomatoes
- 4 tablespoons olive oil, plus more to finish
- 6 garlic cloves, finely minced or grated
- 5 large shallots, minced
- 2 stalks celery, minced
- 1 carrot, minced
- 2 pounds boneless, skinless chicken thighs, finely chopped
- 1 tablespoon minced fresh rosemary
- 3 teaspoons salt
- ½ cup white wine
- 1 (15-ounce) can plus 1 (8-ounce) can tomato sauce
- 1 tablespoon sherry vinegar, to finish
- 1 pound cooked pasta, for serving

My older son once said, "When your mom is a food writer, you don't have comfort foods, because she never makes the same things over and over." I instantly felt defensive, because that's not true.

Well, not *exactly*.

As I started running through dishes that I think of as his comfort foods, we agreed that number one on the list was meat sauce. But then he pointed out that I don't have just one single meat sauce recipe. There's my ground beef meat sauce, my pulled meat sauce that combines beef and pork, and my chicken thigh ragu.

So I guess we were both a little right and a little wrong. But at least he gets to eat a lot of delicious food — and apparently this is his favorite of them all.

1. Place the tomatoes and their juices in a bowl and, using your hands, break up the tomatoes, discarding the tough bits; set aside.

2. Heat 2 tablespoons of the oil in a large pot set over medium heat. Add the garlic, shallots, celery, and carrot, and sauté until the vegetables are soft and fragrant, 5 to 8 minutes.

3. Add the chicken, rosemary, and salt. Cook until the chicken cooks through, about 10 minutes. Turn the heat to medium-high and add the wine; cook until it evaporates, 7 to 8 minutes, periodically breaking up the chicken with the back of a fork or wooden spoon.

4. Add the tomatoes, both cans of tomato sauce, 8 ounces of water used to rinse the smaller can of tomato sauce, and the remaining 2 tablespoons oil. Bring the sauce to a boil, lower the heat to medium-low (or whatever allows it to simmer), and cook until the sauce reaches the desired consistency, about 30 minutes.

5. Remove the pot from the heat and stir in a hearty glug of oil and the vinegar. Season to taste with more salt, if desired. Serve immediately or allow to cool completely before storing in the refrigerator for up to 5 days or in the freezer for up to 3 months.

COOK'S NOTE

For a sauce that cooks so quickly, this is very robustly flavored, but the prep work takes quite a bit of time if you opt to chop everything by hand. I strongly recommend that you use a food processor to finely pulse the chicken.

If you also use a food processor to chop the vegetables, do so before pulsing the chicken. It makes for way easier cleanup. Also note that chopping veggies in a food processor can make them watery. If this happens, they may need to cook longer in step 2.

Green and White Chicken Chili

4–6 servings

INGREDIENTS

- 2 tablespoons neutral oil, such as grapeseed
- 1 large onion, chopped
- 5 garlic cloves, finely minced or grated
- 3 (4½-ounce) cans green chiles, mild, medium, or spicy
- 2 fresh jalapeño chiles, chopped (seeded and deveined for mild)
- 1 tablespoon ground cumin
- 2 teaspoons dried oregano
- 2 teaspoons ground coriander
- 2 pounds ground chicken, preferably dark meat
- 4 cups chicken stock (homemade, page 99, or store-bought)
- 3 (15-ounce) cans cannellini beans, drained and rinsed
- 5 scallions, washed, trimmed, and chopped
- ½ cup chopped fresh cilantro
- ¼ cup lime juice (from about 2 juicy limes)
- 1½ teaspoons salt
- Favorite garnishes, such as grated cheddar cheese, sour cream, and thinly sliced fresh jalapeños
- Tortilla chips, for serving (optional)

When I first started making chili, I followed the most elaborate recipes I could find and experimented with long lists of spices, peppers, beers — you name it. But the more I developed an understanding of what makes a great chili (and the busier life got), the more I realized I could eke out great flavor from a short, simple list of ingredients. This everyday version, with green chiles and white beans, is a perfect example.

1 Heat the oil in a large pot set over medium heat. Add the onion and sauté until fragrant, 3 to 5 minutes. Add the garlic, canned chiles, and jalapeños, and continue cooking for 3 minutes, stirring to keep the vegetables from sticking to the bottom of the pot. Add the cumin, oregano, and coriander. Cook for 1 minute longer, stirring all the while to keep the spices from burning.

2 Add the chicken and cook for about 3 minutes, breaking up the meat all the while. Add approximately 3 cups of the stock and 2 cans of the beans. Stir and allow the chili to come up to a simmer.

In the meantime, add the remaining 1 cup stock and 1 can beans to a blender or to a bowl that can be used with an immersion blender and blend the two together. Once it becomes a smooth mixture, add it to the chili and stir well to incorporate.

3 Adjust the heat as necessary so that the chili can simmer to the desired consistency, 30 to 40 minutes. Be sure to stir occasionally to keep the bottom from burning to the pot. Once done, remove the chili from the heat and stir in the scallions, cilantro, lime juice, and salt. Allow to cool for a few minutes before tasting and adjusting the seasoning as desired. Serve with favorite garnishes and tortilla chips, if desired.

Indian-Style Fried Chicken Thighs

4 servings

INGREDIENTS

- 1 cup buttermilk
- 4 garlic cloves
- ½ cup fresh cilantro, leaves and stems
- ¼ cup fresh mint leaves
- 1-inch knob ginger, peeled and roughly chopped
- 3 tablespoons yellow curry powder
- 6 teaspoons garam masala
- 4 boneless, skinless chicken thighs
- Canola oil (see note, page 114)
- 1 cup all-purpose flour
- ½ cup cornstarch
- 1½ tablespoons salt
- Buttered naan bread or rice, for serving (optional)
- Shredded cabbage, for serving (optional)
- Yogurt raita, for serving (optional)

COOK'S NOTE

You'll need a frying thermometer to monitor the heat of the oil.

Fried chicken may be a plat du jour, but it isn't just classic Southern-style fried chicken that has begun popping up everywhere. Nashville hot chicken, Korean fried chicken, and karaage (Japanese fried chicken usually served at ramen shops) are popular, too. Fried chicken went global, and I have to admit: I am here for it.

This recipe is inspired by the fried chicken that chef Asha Gomez makes on an episode of *Ugly Delicious*, a food docu-series on Netflix hosted by chef David Chang. She doesn't share the recipe on the episode, so I take a few liberties and play with measurements, but the idea and flavor profiles are hers — and totally genius.

1 Add the buttermilk, garlic, cilantro, mint, ginger, 2 tablespoons of the curry powder, and 4 teaspoons of the garam masala to a blender and blend until smooth.

Transfer this marinade and the chicken to a bowl with a lid or to a large food storage bag and seal. Set on the counter to marinate for at least 2 hours or place in the refrigerator for longer, up to overnight.

2 When ready to cook, prepare your frying station: Set a cooling rack on top of a large sheet pan next to the stove. Pour enough oil into a large pot so that it comes 1 inch up the sides. Clip a frying thermometer to the side of your pot.

3 Whisk together the flour, cornstarch, salt, remaining 1 tablespoon curry powder, and remaining 2 teaspoons garam masala in a wide, shallow bowl. Start heating the oil over medium-high heat as you dredge the chicken in the flour mixture to coat well. (I like to do this in batches as the oil is ready so that the coating doesn't get wet before frying from sitting too long on the chicken.)

4 Once the oil reaches around 360°F (180°C), shake excess flour off of a couple of well-coated chicken pieces and drop them in the oil, being careful not to overcrowd the pot (I fry in a pot that is 12 inches in diameter and cook two thighs at a time). Fry each piece for 5 minutes, using tongs to carefully flip the chicken halfway through. Transfer the fried chicken to the cooling rack, immediately sprinkle very lightly with salt, and allow the chicken to rest for 5 minutes.

Repeat until all pieces are fried. If desired, lightly dab the chicken with paper towels to soak up any excess oil before serving with buttery naan bread or rice and thinly shaved cabbage tossed with yogurt raita, if desired.

INGREDIENTS

FOR THE CHICKEN

4 boneless, skinless chicken thighs

1 cup buttermilk

Canola oil (see note, page 114)

1 cup all-purpose flour

½ cup cornstarch

2 tablespoons garlic powder

1 tablespoon salt

1 tablespoon freshly ground black pepper

¼ teaspoon cayenne pepper

FOR THE SANDWICHES

½ cup mayonnaise

2 tablespoons chopped fresh chives

2 teaspoons dill pickle brine

2 teaspoons mustard, preferably Dijon

4 sandwich rolls, preferably potato rolls

Unsalted butter, for the rolls

Iceberg lettuce, preferably shredded, for serving

Sliced tomato, for serving

Dill pickle slices, for serving

My Favorite Fast Food–Style

Fried Chicken Sandwich

If you're going to master chicken, you need to know how to fry it up. But remember: we're curating a handful of fun, vibrant, simple recipes here. So going with bone-in, skin-on pieces for an all-out Sunday-night fried chicken dinner didn't feel right. (Though the method for that isn't much different, except that you'll need more of everything, from flour to oil, and a longer cooking time.)

Borrowing from a more recent fast food history, to which I can speak more honestly (having grown up on the stuff) and that I share with my kids (who are obsessed with the Shake Shack chicken sandwich, and now with this recipe, too), I decided to go with a fried chicken sandwich instead. Plus, the combination of shredded lettuce, pickles, and special sauce gets me every time. Feel free to put your own twist on this sandwich.

1 **MAKE THE CHICKEN:** Add the chicken and buttermilk to a bowl with a lid or to a large food storage bag and seal. Set on the counter to marinate for 1 hour or place in the refrigerator for longer, up to overnight.

If you don't have even an hour to spare for marinating, you can use the buttermilk as a dip before dredging the meat in flour, skipping this step altogether. The chicken will not be quite as tender, but it will still be juicy and delicious.

2 When ready to cook, prepare your frying station: Set a cooling rack on top of a large sheet pan next to the stove. Pour enough oil into a large pot so that it comes 1 inch up the sides. Clip a frying thermometer to the side of your pot.

3 Whisk together the flour, cornstarch, garlic powder, salt, black pepper, and cayenne in a wide, shallow bowl. Start heating the oil over medium-high heat as you dredge the chicken in the flour mixture to coat well. (I like to do this in batches as the oil is ready so that the coating doesn't get wet before frying from sitting too long on the chicken.)

4 Once the oil reaches around 360°F (180°C), shake excess flour off of a couple of chicken pieces and drop them in the oil, being careful not to overcrowd the pot (I fry in a pot that is 12 inches in diameter and cook two thighs at a time). Fry for 5 minutes, using tongs to carefully flip the pieces halfway through.

COOK'S NOTE

You'll need a frying thermometer to monitor the heat of the oil.

Transfer the fried chicken to the cooling rack, and allow it to rest for 5 minutes. Repeat until all pieces are done. If desired, lightly dab the chicken with paper towels to soak up any excess oil before serving.

5 **MAKE THE SANDWICHES:** To make the sauce, whisk together the mayonnaise, chives, pickle brine, and mustard. If not assembling the sandwiches right away, set the sauce aside in the refrigerator.

6 Toast the rolls and butter both sides. Slather the top half of each roll with sauce. Place a chicken thigh on the bottom half of each roll and top with lettuce, sliced tomato, and dill pickle. Add the top half and serve immediately.

FRIED CHICKEN
THAT RULES THE ROOST

The truth is, even simple fried chicken — dipped for a minute in buttermilk and coated with nothing more than salt-and-pepper-seasoned flour — can be utterly delicious. So while soaking and brines, spices and coatings, can make or break a recipe, they aren't the be-all and end-all. But cooking your chicken at the right temperature can be.

Even a delicious recipe can turn into a soggy mess if you fry your chicken at too low a temperature or allow the temperature to fluctuate too much during the frying process. So it's critical to make sure that your canola oil gets to at least 360°F (180°C) before you start — because the temperature will drop as soon as you add chicken to the pot — and to keep a watchful eye on maintaining an oil temp of around 350°F (180°C) the entire time that you're frying.

Note: If you don't have canola oil, vegetable shortening is a great alternative and should also be maintained at 360°F while frying. (Some say vegetable shortening is a *better* option, but I suggest canola since it's more readily available in most pantries; if you have vegetable shortening on hand, feel free to try it out of the gate.) Other oils that work for frying chicken at high heat include grapeseed, vegetable, and peanut oil. Just be sure to look up their frying temperatures before you begin so that you can ensure a crispy crust.

4 servings

INGREDIENTS

FOR THE CHICKEN

2 garlic cloves

1 small onion, roughly chopped

1 cup roughly chopped fresh pineapple (from about ½ a whole, fresh pineapple; you can substitute canned, but it's not nearly as delicious)

2 teaspoons ground cumin

1 teaspoon chili powder

1½ pounds boneless, skinless chicken breasts (see note, page 117)

1½ teaspoons salt

½ teaspoon freshly ground black pepper

FOR THE SALAD

1 pound fresh green beans, trimmed

½ cup unsweetened shredded coconut

2 shallots, thinly sliced

⅔ cup neutral oil, such as grapeseed

Salt

1 garlic clove

¼ cup lime juice (from about 2 juicy limes)

1 jalapeño, roughly chopped (seeded and deveined for mild)

2 teaspoons fresh thyme, roughly chopped

1½ teaspoons honey

1 teaspoon ground allspice

1 cup cilantro, roughly chopped

Freshly ground black pepper

1 red Fresno chile, thinly sliced, for garnish (you can substitute red jalapeño; optional)

Pineapple Chicken Salad
with Green Beans and Toasted Coconut

This salad was inspired by one of my favorite choices at Lemonade, a healthy, fast-casual restaurant chain that I sometimes visit when in Los Angeles. I enjoy it so much that as soon as I agreed to work on this book, I attempted to re-create the flavors.

I thought the exercise would be just for fun, to get into the swing of the project. Little did I know that my family would go crazy for this and insist that I make the recipe a keeper. If you love it, too, you have them to thank for it.

1 **MAKE THE CHICKEN:** Add the garlic, onion, pineapple, cumin, and chili powder to a blender or a food processor and purée until it is the consistency of applesauce.

Add the chicken breasts to the insert of your electric pressure cooker and pour the pineapple purée over the top. Set the pressure cooker to high for 18 minutes and cover, remembering to set the valve on the lid to *pressure*. When done cooking, manually release the pressure valve. Once cool enough to handle, shred the cooked chicken and season with the salt and pepper; set aside.

2 **MAKE THE SALAD:** While the chicken cooks, steam the green beans until tender crisp. Once cool enough to handle, cut them into roughly 1-inch pieces; set aside.

3 Add the coconut to a small sauté pan set over medium-high heat. Leave it untouched until it just begins to turn golden brown around the edges, about 1 minute, watching carefully all the while. Then, using a wooden spoon or silicone spatula, toss the coconut constantly until all of it turns a deep golden brown, another 30 seconds or so. Remove the coconut from the heat and transfer it to a small bowl; set aside.

Recipe continues on page 117

COOK'S NOTE

To cook on the stovetop, use the smallest pot that allows you to lay the chicken in a single layer. Cover with the pineapple sauce and add just enough chicken broth (you can use water in a pinch) to cover the chicken by about 1 inch. Cook on medium-low for 20 to 25 minutes.

Remove the chicken from the pot and allow it to cool before shredding. In the meantime, reduce the sauce on medium until you have enough to coat the pulled chicken without it being overly saucy. Because you've added liquid to the recipe, you may also need to adjust the seasoning. Reducing the sauce helps concentrate the flavor, but taste as you go.

4 Wipe the pan clean and return it to the stove. Set a paper towel–lined plate next to the stove. Add the shallots and ⅓ cup of the oil to the pan and set over medium heat. Cook, stirring frequently, until they crisp and turn a deep golden brown, 12 to 15 minutes. Using a slotted spoon, transfer the shallots to the prepared plate, sprinkle with salt to taste, and allow them to rest.

5 To make the dressing: Roughly chop the garlic and add it to a blender along with the lime juice, jalapeño, thyme, honey, and allspice, and blend until smooth, stopping to scrape down the sides as necessary. Leave the blender running and add the remaining ⅓ cup oil in a slow, steady stream until the dressing emulsifies.

6 Place the chicken, green beans, coconut, shallots, and ¼ cup of the cilantro in a large serving bowl. Toss with the dressing and season to taste with salt and black pepper, if desired. Top with the remaining ¾ cup cilantro and the thinly sliced chiles, if using. Serve immediately or at room temperature.

Shredded Harissa Chicken

4 servings

INGREDIENTS

- 2 tablespoons olive oil, plus more for serving
- 2 garlic cloves, roughly chopped
- 2 tablespoons ground coriander
- 1 tablespoon ground cumin
- 1 tablespoon smoked paprika
- 2 tablespoons tomato paste
- 1 (12-ounce) jar roasted red peppers, drained
- 2 tablespoons lemon juice (from about 1 juicy lemon), plus more for serving
- ¾–1 teaspoon salt
- 2 pounds boneless, skinless chicken thighs
- Couscous, white rice, or rice pilaf, for serving (optional)
- Tzatziki (homemade, page 59, or store-bought) or feta cheese, for serving (optional)
- Halved or quartered cherry tomatoes, for serving (optional)

To be completely honest, I take a major liberty by naming harissa in this recipe. What I make here is just barely an approximation of the smoky, spicy, seductive chili paste of North Africa, most commonly associated with Tunisia.

A real harissa is thicker and much more complex. It can be a little much for my kids, but I liked the idea of introducing them to the basic flavor profile and, in doing so, I hit on this dinner that's become a weeknight staple.

1 Heat the oil in a small pan set over medium heat. Once the oil begins to shimmer, add the garlic and sauté until it just begins to turn golden brown, 1 to 2 minutes. Add the coriander, cumin, and paprika, and toast, stirring constantly, until they turn one shade darker brown, 1½ minutes. Add the tomato paste and, continuing to stir constantly, cook until the mixture comes together, about 30 seconds. Immediately remove the paste from the hot pan so that it does not burn.

2 Add the paste to a high-powered blender or food processor along with the peppers, lemon juice, and ½ teaspoon of the salt, and blend to the desired consistency. (I like this sauce with a little bit of texture, so I either pulse it three times in a high-powered blender and then let it run for 30 seconds at low, or I let it run for 10 to 15 seconds in a food processor. Play with it until you get a consistency that you like.)

3 Add the chicken thighs to the insert of your electric pressure cooker and pour the sauce over them; toss to coat. Set the pressure cooker to high for 18 minutes and cover, remembering to set the valve on the lid to *pressure*. When done cooking, manually release the pressure valve. Once cool enough to handle, shred the chicken and season to taste with the remaining ¼ to ½ teaspoon salt, adding more if desired. Serve piled over couscous and topped with tzatziki or feta cheese and tomatoes if desired, plus a squeeze of lemon juice and a drizzle of oil.

COOK'S NOTE

To cook on the stovetop, use the smallest pot that allows you to lay the chicken in a single layer. Cover with the harissa sauce and add just enough chicken broth (you can use water in a pinch) to cover the chicken by about 1 inch. Cook on medium-low for 20 to 25 minutes.

Remove the chicken from the pot and allow it to cool before shredding. In the meantime, reduce the sauce on medium until you have enough to coat the pulled chicken without it being overly saucy. Because you've added liquid to the recipe, you may also need to adjust the seasoning. Reducing the sauce helps concentrate the flavor, but taste as you go.

Butter Chicken

4 servings

INGREDIENTS

FOR THE MARINADE

¾ cup plain Greek-style yogurt

3 garlic cloves, minced or grated

3 tablespoons minced or grated fresh turmeric (or substitute 1 tablespoon ground turmeric)

1 tablespoon lemon juice (from about 1 juicy lemon)

2 teaspoons garam masala

2 pounds boneless, skinless chicken breasts, cut into 2-inch chunks

FOR THE CHICKEN

½ cup heavy cream

4 tablespoons unsalted butter

2 tablespoons neutral oil, such as grapeseed

1 cinnamon stick

1 tablespoon minced or grated fresh ginger

1 green chile, halved lengthwise (optional)

5 garlic cloves, minced or grated

3 tablespoons tomato paste

1 tablespoon garam masala

1 teaspoon paprika

¼ teaspoon ground cardamom

1 (14-ounce) can crushed tomatoes

2 teaspoons honey

1 teaspoon salt

Lemon juice, to taste

Fresh cilantro, for garnish (optional)

Steamed basmati rice, for serving (optional)

I'm that person who never wants to order the same thing twice — except when it comes to my Indian food take-out order. If we eat at an Indian restaurant, I'm always game for a new dish. But it's hard to resist this comfort dish when we order takeout, so I decided to try my hand at creating a homemade version.

If you read the section on marinating (page 126), you might wonder why boneless, skinless chicken can sit in this marinade, made with acidic lemon and yogurt, for up to 24 hours. The calcium in dairy makes the difference: it helps tenderize chicken. Plus yogurt isn't nearly as acidic as vinegar or citrus, and there's only a small amount of lemon juice, so it works.

1 **MAKE THE MARINADE:** Whisk together the yogurt, garlic, turmeric, lemon juice, and garam masala in a medium bowl. Add it and the chicken to a bowl with a lid or to a large food storage bag and seal. Set on the counter to marinate for at least 2 hours or place in the refrigerator for longer, up to overnight.

2 **MAKE THE CHICKEN:** If you have time, remove the chicken from your refrigerator up to 1 hour before cooking. Also take the cream out of the refrigerator to allow it to come to room temperature.

Set the electric pressure cooker to *sauté* for 15 minutes. Add the butter, oil, cinnamon stick, ginger, and chile, if using. Cook for about 3 minutes, stirring occasionally. If you don't want to add much heat — especially if you've used a spicier chile — remove the chile before moving on to the next step.

3 Add the garlic, tomato paste, garam masala, paprika, and cardamom. Cook the spices until fragrant, stirring constantly with a wooden spoon or silicone spatula to keep the mixture from burning, 1½ to 2 minutes. Add the chicken, shaking off excess marinade before placing it in the insert of the pressure cooker, and sauté for 3 to 4 minutes, turning the pieces at least once. At this point, time on the *sauté* function should be close to running out or have run out altogether.

4 Add the tomatoes, set the pressure cooker to low for 5 minutes, and cover, remembering to set the valve on the lid to *pressure*. When done cooking, allow the pressure valve to release naturally.

   Once you're able to uncover the pressure cooker, pour the cream into a medium bowl and carefully spoon small amounts of the hot sauce into the cream to temper it, stirring between each addition. Once you've added enough hot sauce to make the cream very warm to the touch, pour it into the insert. Add the honey and salt; stir and season to taste with lemon juice and more salt, if desired. Serve topped with cilantro with steamed basmati rice, if desired.

COOK'S NOTE

To cook on the stovetop, add ½ cup chicken broth (you can use water in a pinch) along with the tomatoes in step 4. Bring the whole pot just to a boil, then lower the heat to simmer for 15 minutes. Proceed by adding the cream, honey, salt, and lemon juice as directed.

Filipino-Style Chicken Adobo

4 servings

INGREDIENTS

- 1 cup distilled white vinegar
- ⅔ cup low-sodium soy sauce
- 10 garlic cloves, peeled and trimmed
- 4 bay leaves
- 2 tablespoons dark brown or light brown sugar
- ¼ teaspoon whole black peppercorns
- 1 whole chicken (3½ to 4 pounds), cut into pieces

  Steamed white rice, for serving (optional)

COOK'S NOTE

To cook on the stovetop, adjust the cooking time to 40 minutes. For falling-off-the-bone chicken, cook it even longer. This recipe is really flexible: just keep an eye on the sauce to make sure that it doesn't reduce too much. You'll want to have plenty for serving over the meat and rice.

Other than butter, two ingredients at the top of my favorites list are salt and vinegar. So there was no way that I could write a chicken cookbook that didn't include Filipino-style chicken adobo given that it's flavored almost entirely by soy sauce (which is basically salt) and vinegar. It's a no-brainer. Plus, making it in an electric pressure cooker, you end up with totally delicious, falling-off-the-bone meat.

Even though chicken (and pork) adobo are usually stewed, the meat is often crisped right before serving. In this recipe, I use the broiler to help. And if I happen to have leftovers, I use my fingers to pull off the skin, which will just get soggy once packed overnight, and pick the meat from the bone, which takes hardly any effort. I save what's left in a pool of syrupy sauce to eat over reheated white rice later that week.

Or more likely, the next day.

1 Combine the vinegar, soy sauce, garlic, bay leaves, sugar, and peppercorns in a medium bowl, stirring until the sugar dissolves. Add this marinade and the chicken to a bowl with a lid or to a large food storage bag and seal. Set on the counter to marinate for at least 2 hours or place in the refrigerator for longer, up to overnight.

2 When ready to cook, add the chicken and the marinade to the insert of your electric pressure cooker; adjust the chicken as necessary so that it is in as much of a single layer as possible, covered by as much of the marinade as possible. Set the pressure cooker to high for 12 minutes and cover, remembering to set the valve on the lid to *pressure*. When done cooking, allow the pressure valve to release naturally.

3 While you wait for the pressure cooker to release, preheat the broiler to low. Once you're able to remove the lid from the pressure cooker, transfer the chicken skin side up to a sheet pan, and place under the broiler to crisp the skin, about 5 minutes, watching carefully so that it does not burn. Allow the chicken to rest for 10 minutes.

4 While the chicken broils and rests, reduce the sauce: Reset the pressure cooker to *sauté* for 15 minutes. Allow the sauce to cook down, stirring occasionally. After 15 minutes, turn the pressure cooker off and strain the sauce, discarding the bay leaves and peppercorns; you can choose to mash the garlic cloves into your sauce or not. If desired, serve the chicken over rice with the sauce spooned over the top.

ON A GRILL
Burgers & Wings

There's something wonderfully primal about grilling: it's just food and fire, like how I imagine it was when we lived in hunter-gatherer times. But as it turns out, primal does not necessarily mean without margins of error. Though simple, grilling can go wrong.

The challenge with grilling is finding a way to cook the inside of a piece of meat all the way through without completely incinerating the outside with the high heat of the flame. It turns out that the best way to do this is to sear the outside with a high flame, then reduce the flame and close the grill to finish cooking.

When cooked this way, chicken remains juicy and tender, with a great flame-broiled taste from a good sear. Then, it's just up to you to add some extra flavor using a brine, rub, sauce, or marinade.

BRINES, SAUCES, RUBS, AND MARINADES

THE SIMPLEST WAY to ensure that your chicken stays tender and full of flavor on the grill is to wet brine it for an hour before cooking (page 48; add sugar to accelerate caramelization for your sear). Even if you add garlic, herbs, and spices to your brine, you'll still get a pure chicken flavor from a simply brined bird cooked on the grill. If you're looking for something more, you can combine brining with a wet sauce (e.g., BBQ sauce) that's brushed on during cooking.

Another option is to dry brine (page 50; also with sugar added to accelerate caramelization during grilling) or use a spice rub, which can be massaged onto the meat an hour ahead of time or even right before grilling.

Lastly, you can marinate your chicken. Marinades are the trickiest — and sometimes the most work intensive — of the options, but strangely, the most popular.

ALL ABOUT MARINADES

YOU CAN MARINATE CHICKEN no matter how you plan to cook it, but doing so is especially great for grilled chicken. Like brining, there are many opinions — and lots of conflicting scientific claims — about marinating; in particular, using marinades with acids like vinegar, lemon, and other citrus juices. Also like brining, I'm going to spare you too many details. But here's what I can tell you for sure:

Highly acidic marinades can cause chicken, especially boneless, skinless chicken, to get mealy if it sits too long. And by too long I mean 24 hours, which is a common recommendation.

Having learned the hard way, I've come to avoid highly acidic marinades almost completely for long soaks. Instead, I either keep the acidity of my marinades low or I skip the acid altogether, using only a combination of oil, fresh herbs, dried spices, aromatics, and fun stuff like jam, Sriracha, soy sauce, honey,

or mustard. I add acid to some reserved marinade for basting while cooking.

On the other hand, when I want to use a highly acidic marinade — like for superlemony Greek-style chicken — I limit the amount of time that my chicken sits. Boneless, skinless cuts can soak for as little as 20 to 60 minutes and still have tons of flavor! In fact, even though most recipes still suggest allowing chicken to sit for up to overnight, a 2-hour soak is usually fine for most marinades, acidic or not, especially with boneless, skinless cuts. I only suggest up to overnight in some cases in this book because 2 hours is not all that practical.

Oh, and before you get too nervous about acidic marinades and mealy chicken, keep in mind that when the acidity level of the marinade is low, letting chicken sit for 24 hours won't cause a major problem. This is all just good to know as a rule of thumb.

FIVE OF MY FAVORITE EASY MARINADES

ONE

Honey Mustard

⅓ cup mustard
   (a combination of
   Dijon and grainy is
   preferable)

¼ cup honey

3 tablespoons
   olive oil

2 tablespoons apple
   cider vinegar

TWO

Lemony Oregano

½ cup lemon juice (from about 8 juicy
   lemons)

¼ cup water

¼ cup olive oil

1 tablespoon fine sea salt

1 tablespoon dried oregano

1 teaspoon lemon zest

Marinate the chicken for 20 to 60 minutes at
room temperature, erring on the quick side for
boneless, skinless cuts.

THREE

Orange–Chipotle

¾ cup adobo sauce
   from a can of
   chipotles in adobo

¼ cup mayonnaise

3 tablespoons
   orange juice

2 tablespoons pure
   maple syrup

1 teaspoon salt

Each recipe makes 1 cup. Whisk all of the ingredients together. With all but the Lemony Oregano, you can marinate chicken for anywhere from 2 hours at room temperature up to overnight in the refrigerator. Season the chicken with salt before cooking.

FOUR

Ranch

- 1 cup buttermilk
- 3 large garlic cloves, chopped
- 2 tablespoons finely chopped shallot
- 1 tablespoon vinegar-based hot sauce, such as Frank's RedHot
- 1 teaspoon onion powder
- 1 teaspoon salt
- ½ teaspoon dried dill

FIVE

Soy-Lime

- ¼ cup neutral oil, such as grapeseed
- ¼ cup soy sauce (low sodium preferred)
- 3 tablespoons lime juice (from about 1½ juicy limes)
- 2 tablespoons fish sauce
- 2 tablespoons finely chopped shallot
- 2 tablespoons light brown sugar
- 1 tablespoon grated fresh ginger

Pepper Jack Guacamole Burgers

4 servings

INGREDIENTS

- 1 tablespoon neutral oil, such as grapeseed, plus more for brushing the grill

- 1½ pounds ground chicken (preferably 1 pound white meat plus ½ pound dark meat)

- ½ cup (2 ounces) shredded pepper Jack cheese

- ¼ cup finely chopped scallions, white and green parts (from about 2 scallions)

- 1 teaspoon garlic powder

- ½ teaspoon ground cumin

- ½ teaspoon salt

- ¼ teaspoon freshly ground black pepper

- 4 toasted rolls

- Lettuce, for serving

- Guacamole, for serving

- Sliced red onion, for serving

- Sliced tomato, for serving (you can substitute fresh pico de gallo)

The Thai Chicken Burgers in my first cookbook, *Make It Easy*, are one of my kids' favorite recipes of all time, so I knew that I had to make the chicken burgers for this book *really* good. On the search for a slam-dunk dinner, I decided to draw inspiration from their favorite snack, guac and chips.

I started experimenting by combining ground chicken with salsa ingredients like fresh onion and garlic. I even added pico de gallo in one pass. But once the cooked burger is all decked out, with a bun and guacamole on top, the flavor of those fresh ingredients didn't hold up like this simple combination of fresh scallion, strong ground spices, and grated pepper Jack cheese. And what a boon, since it makes prep even easier.

1 Preheat the grill to medium and brush with oil. In the meantime, add the oil, chicken, cheese, scallions, garlic powder, cumin, salt, and pepper to a medium bowl. Use your hands to combine well, being careful not to overmix, which can make the burgers tough.

2 Lightly wet your hands before forming the mixture into four equal patties, each about ½ inch thick. Grill until cooked through, 5 to 7 minutes per side. (You can also cook these in the broiler or in a large, oiled skillet set over medium heat for about the same time.) Allow the burgers to rest for 5 minutes before serving on toasted rolls topped with lettuce, guacamole, red onion, and tomato. When tomatoes are out of season, or whenever you prefer, use pico de gallo instead.

COOK'S NOTE

Unlike beef and other red meat, ground chicken can get very sticky. When forming patties, keep your hands very slightly damp to help keep the chicken from sticking to them.

THE BIG CHEESE TREATMENT

Preshredded cheese can be a lifesaver, I know, but I strongly suggest that you grate your own pepper Jack for these burgers. Doing so for only 2 ounces will take all of five minutes (estimate about one-fourth of an 8-ounce block). Cheese that you've grated yourself — especially if you use a rasp grater — will melt beautifully and help keep your burgers supermoist, even if you overcook them a little bit.

Which I'm sure you won't.

Jerk Chicken

4 servings

INGREDIENTS

- 4 scallions, each trimmed and cut into 4 pieces
- 4 garlic cloves, peeled, trimmed, and smashed
- 2 hot chiles, such as jalapeños, habaneros, or more traditional scotch bonnets (listed from least to most spicy; gauge your family's tolerance accordingly)
- ½ large onion, roughly chopped
- 1-inch knob ginger, peeled and roughly chopped
- ¼ cup lime juice (from about 2 juicy limes)
- 3 tablespoons soy sauce
- 4 teaspoons freshly ground black pepper
- 1 tablespoon neutral oil, such as grapeseed, plus more for brushing the grill
- 1 tablespoon dark brown or light brown sugar
- 1 tablespoon ground allspice
- 2 teaspoons fresh thyme
- 1 teaspoon ground nutmeg (freshly grated preferred)
- 1 teaspoon salt
- Pinch of ground cloves
- 4 bone-in, skin-on chicken leg quarters, split

One of my older son's first favorite foods was spicy jerk pork and chicken. Our friend Jenny, who took care of him for years, is from Jamaica and would bring him tastes of a family recipe. He fell in love instantly, heat and all. It was such a hit that one time she even had a heavenly hunk of smoky jerk pork FedExed to our house!

My version is delicious, though I'm not sure it will ever quite measure up. Between Jenny's visits — and until we can visit her in her hometown — this version tides us over.

1 Add the scallions, garlic, chiles, onion, ginger, lime juice, soy sauce, pepper, oil, sugar, allspice, thyme, nutmeg, salt, and cloves to a blender, and blend until smooth. Set aside ¼ cup of the marinade (on the counter if cooking the chicken within 2 hours or in the refrigerator otherwise). Place the remaining marinade and the chicken in a bowl with a lid or in a large food storage bag and seal. Set on the counter to marinate for at least 2 hours or place in the refrigerator for longer, up to overnight.

2 When ready to cook, preheat the grill to high and brush with oil. If the chicken was in the refrigerator, allow it to come to room temperature before cooking, if you have time. Place the chicken on the grill and char on all sides, turning and basting with the reserved marinade every minute or so, for about 5 minutes total.

3 Reduce the heat to medium-low and cover. Grill, continuing to baste every 5 minutes, until the chicken is fully cooked: an instant-read thermometer should register 165°F (75°C) at the thickest part of both the legs and thighs. This should take 15 to 18 minutes for the legs, and 10 to 15 minutes for the thighs. Serve immediately or at room temperature.

COOK'S NOTES

If you have the time to dry brine, you won't regret it. Follow the directions on page 51 and skip the salt in this recipe.

Split leg quarters are usually sold at supermarkets as "chicken drumsticks and thighs," with one package containing two drumsticks and two thighs. Alternatively, you may have to buy the bone-in, skin-on drumsticks and thighs separately, or you can buy whole leg quarters (the drumsticks and thighs still connected) and split them in half yourself (see page 28). You need four drumsticks and four thighs, total, for this recipe.

Peachy Sriracha Sticky Wings

INGREDIENTS

- 1 cup peach jam or preserves
- 2 tablespoons Sriracha, plus more for spicier wings (see headnote)
- 1 tablespoon neutral oil, such as grapeseed, plus more for brushing the grill
- 1 teaspoon fish sauce
- ½ teaspoon salt
- 2 teaspoons unseasoned rice wine vinegar
- 3 pounds chicken wings, wing tips removed and remaining wings split in two at the joint (page 26)
- Freshly ground black pepper

If you ask me, wings are meant to be a simple pleasure. I'm happy as long as they taste good, are easy to make, and hit these three marks: Spicy. Sticky. Messy.

If that's enough to satisfy you, too, you'll also love this simple, sweet-and-just-a-little-spicy recipe. If you want more than just a little spicy, simply add more Sriracha. That's what I do when my kids are not around.

1 Whisk together the peach jam, Sriracha, oil, fish sauce, and salt in a medium bowl until smooth. Separate ¼ cup of the marinade and mix the vinegar into this reserve; set the reserve aside on the counter if cooking the wings within 2 hours or in the refrigerator if not cooking them until later.

2 Add the larger portion of the marinade and the chicken to a bowl with a lid or to a large food storage bag and seal. Set on the counter to marinate for at least 2 hours or place in the refrigerator for longer, up to overnight.

3 When ready to cook, preheat the grill to medium-high and brush with oil. If the chicken was in the refrigerator, allow it to come to room temperature, if you have time. Place the wings on the grill and season generously with salt and pepper. Cook uncovered, turning and basting with the reserved marinade every 5 minutes, until crispy around the edges and cooked through, about 18 minutes. Season to taste with more salt and pepper, if desired, and serve immediately.

WINGS IN THE OVEN

I don't need to tell you that wings cooked on the grill are things of beauty, but if you don't have a grill or it's raining, here's how you can cook them in the oven.

In step 3, preheat your oven to 400°F (200°C). In the meantime, line a large sheet pan with aluminum foil for easy cleanup and place a rack on top. Spray or wipe the rack with oil to keep the wings from sticking.

Place the wings on the rack skin side down, season with salt and pepper, and pop them in the oven. Set a master timer for 30 minutes total cook time. After the first 10 minutes, baste with the reserved marinade. After another 10 minutes, flip and baste the wings again. Season with more salt and pepper. After the final 10 minutes of cooking, transfer the wings to the broiler and crisp for 3 to 5 minutes, watching carefully to ensure that they don't burn.

Grilled Chicken and Mango Salad

4 servings

INGREDIENTS

FOR THE MARINADE/ DRESSING

- 1 large mango, peeled, pitted, and roughly chopped (about 1 cup)
- ½ jalapeño (seeded and deveined for mild)
- ¼ cup lime juice (from about 2 juicy limes)
- 2 tablespoons orange juice
- 2 tablespoons apple cider vinegar
- 1 teaspoon salt
- ¼ cup neutral oil, such as grapeseed
- 3 large boneless, skinless chicken breasts

FOR THE SALAD

- 5 shallots, thinly sliced
- 1 cup canola oil, plus more for brushing the grill
- 1 (10-ounce) clamshell or bag washed salad greens
- 1½ red bell peppers, cut into 1-inch-thick strips
- 1 large mango, peeled, pitted, and cut into 1-inch cubes
- ½ English cucumber, cut into 1-inch dice
- ½ cup crumbled queso fresco
- Salt
- Freshly ground black pepper

Grilled chicken on top of salad is about as standard as fare gets. And — let's be honest — about as boring as it gets, too. But there's good reason why it's such a popular option: when done right, a hearty salad with lean, grilled protein like chicken can feel satisfying and healthful at once. It's just hard to do well.

Here's my attempt. And I only call it an attempt because, well, with queso and fried shallots, this doesn't quite qualify as a spa salad. Still, it's healthy enough and the flavor is great. And as a dinner, it's definitely lighter.

In fact, I think it's light enough that you should serve it with a side of rice, beans, and sliced avocado. But that's just me.

1 **MAKE THE MARINADE:** Add the mango, jalapeño, lime juice, orange juice, vinegar, and salt to a blender, and blend until combined. With the motor running, add the oil in a slow, steady stream until the dressing emulsifies. Season to taste with more salt, if desired.

You should end up with about 1½ cups; split this into two equal ¾-cup portions. Set one portion aside as salad dressing, and add the boneless, skinless chicken breasts to the other portion to marinate, sealed, for up to 2 hours at room temperature.

2 When ready to grill the chicken, preheat the grill to medium-high and brush with oil. Grill until the breasts are cooked through, about 10 minutes, flipping once halfway through the cooking time; an instant-read thermometer should register 160°F (70°C) at the thickest part. If not cooked all the way through,

reduce the heat to medium-low, close the grill, and cook for a few minutes longer, until done. Allow the chicken to rest for at least 5 minutes before cutting into thin slices on the bias.

3 **MAKE THE SALAD:** While the chicken marinates or cooks, fry the shallots: Set a paper towel–lined plate next to the stove. Add the shallots and oil to a small pot and set over medium heat. Cook, stirring frequently, until they crisp and turn deep golden brown, 12 to 15 minutes. Using a slotted spoon, transfer the shallots to the prepped plate to rest.

4 Add the greens to a large serving bowl. Toss with the bell peppers, mango, cucumber, cheese, and reserved dressing. Top with the sliced chicken and fried shallots. Season to taste with salt and black pepper as desired. Serve immediately.

BBQ Chicken Pizza

Two 6-inch pies

INGREDIENTS

1 round pizza dough, homemade or store-bought

Olive oil, for brushing

1 cup shredded chicken (see headnote)

½ cup favorite BBQ sauce, homemade or store-bought

All-purpose flour, for dusting

8–16 ounces fresh mozzarella cheese, torn into pieces

¾ cup shredded sharp cheddar or smoked Gouda cheese

¼ red onion, very thinly sliced

Fresh raw corn, for garnish (from 1 cob, when in season; optional)

Fresh cilantro, for garnish (optional)

This recipe is a bit of a cheat because the chicken isn't what's grilled: the pizza is. But hey, knowing how to grill pizza is a life skill, so let's call it a bonus!

You can use any shredded chicken you want here, even store-bought rotisserie (though, c'mon, you're holding a cookbook dedicated to chicken). I usually make this with leftover chicken from my Crazy Delicious Classic Roast Chicken (page 53) or with Poached Chicken (page 142) that I have hanging around.

1 Remove the pizza dough from the refrigerator and allow it to come to room temperature; this will make it much easier to work with.

When ready to cook, preheat your grill to high and brush it with oil. Toss the chicken with ¼ cup of the BBQ sauce and set aside.

2 When the dough is ready, divide it into two even halves. Lightly flour a work surface and, using your hands, gently ease each portion of dough into 6-inch rounds (that don't actually have to be round; irregular is fine). Lightly oil both sides of each round of dough and transfer to a large sheet pan.

3 Slide both rounds onto the grill, close, and cook until the sides facing down are golden brown and have char marks, 1 to 2 minutes. The dough is done when it releases effortlessly. Flip and repeat.

4 Spread the remaining ¼ cup BBQ sauce in a thin layer on top of each pizza, dividing the sauce evenly between the two pies and leaving an inch or so around the edges to create a crust. Top the pizzas with the chicken, mozzarella, cheddar, onion, and corn, if using, being sure to spread the toppings evenly across the sauce and between the pies. Close the grill, turn off the heat, and cook until the cheese melts, another 3 to 5 minutes.

Allow the pizzas to rest for 3 minutes before topping with cilantro (if using), cutting, and serving.

Using & Creating
LEFTOVERS

I used to hate leftovers, but that's because I thought of them as nothing more than round two of the same old thing. And I still hate that. I always prefer something new, and as I've become a more sophisticated home cook, I've come to realize that's exactly what smart leftovers are about. So that's what this chapter is about: how to take leftover chicken from one meal and turn it into something new for another without much effort.

It's also about creating leftovers on purpose. I've included two methods of poaching chicken here, because poaching is easy and produces delicious results. With simply cooked (and sometimes flavored) pulled, chopped, or sliced poached chicken waiting in the fridge, a quick meal can be just minutes away.

Once you get the hang of knowing how to use or create leftovers like this, you're golden. You get to be creative about dinner, with most of the cooking already done. What could be better?

POACHED CHICKEN

BONE-IN, SKIN-ON CHICKEN BREASTS ARE THE IDEAL CUT for juicy poached chicken, but sometimes throwing a couple of boneless, skinless breasts into a pot with cold water (or stock, or milk, or coconut milk) with fresh herbs and aromatics is the path of least resistance to dinner or meal prep for a busy week ahead.

If you're going to poach chicken pieces from a bird that you break down yourself, it'll definitely be easier to keep the bone in and skin on for poaching. They will yield juicier meat, and it will be easier to remove both once cooked. If you're picking up already butchered pieces at the market, it's likely that bone-in, skin-on will be more affordable and, again, they're the better option. But if you've already got boneless, skinless breasts on hand or that's all you can find at the market, they'll work out great, too.

POACHING POSSIBILITIES

There are a few elements of my master poaching recipes that shouldn't be messed with:

- Start with cold water.

- Start low and go slow. Timing matters.

- Add salt.

Beyond that, the possibilities are endless. By now you know that I'm going to encourage you to play with your favorite flavors. A few of mine include:

- White wine and chopped leeks added to the master recipe (a delicious twist on the classic and perfect for fancy salads)

- Sautéed sliced ginger, sliced fresh scallion, and a whole star anise seed added to cooking liquid made with soy sauce, water, and some sugar (great for dishes with a Chinese flavor profile)

- Sliced fresh scallion and curry powder added to coconut milk (gives a nice Indian or Southeast Asian flair)

- Chopped fresh tarragon (very simple and very French)

Poached Boneless, Skinless Chicken Breast

Makes about 2 cups shredded or cubed chicken

INGREDIENTS

1–1½ pounds boneless, skinless chicken breasts

1 teaspoon salt

2 bay leaves

1 garlic clove, peeled and smashed

1 large carrot, roughly cut into 3 pieces

½ teaspoon whole black peppercorns

½ teaspoon whole coriander seeds (optional)

1 Place the chicken breasts in a medium pot in a single layer and sprinkle them with the salt. Add the bay leaves, garlic, carrot, peppercorns, and coriander seeds, if using, along with enough cold water to cover the chicken by about 1 inch.

2 Set the pot over medium-low heat and cook until bubbles begin to form around the edges. Once they do, reduce the heat to low to make sure that the cooking water maintains a temperature between 170 and 180°F (77–82°C). Cook until the chicken is cooked all the way through, 6 to 8 minutes; an instant-read thermometer should register 160°F (70°C) at the thickest part of the breast. If it's not cooked through, cook it longer, checking it every 1 to 2 minutes.

3 Turn the heat off and immediately remove the chicken from the pot, reserving the poaching liquid. Allow the meat to rest and, once cool enough to handle, cut or shred the meat as desired. If not using immediately, pack the chicken in a sealed container with enough poaching liquid to cover it to help keep it moist, and store in the refrigerator for up to 5 days.

Poached Bone-In, Skin-On Chicken Breast

Makes about 4 cups shredded or cubed chicken

INGREDIENTS

3–3½ pounds bone-in, skin-on chicken breasts, whole or split

1 teaspoon salt

2 bay leaves

1 garlic clove, peeled and smashed

1 large carrot, roughly cut into 3 pieces

½ teaspoon whole black peppercorns

½ teaspoon whole coriander seeds (optional)

1 Place the chicken in a medium to large pot (in a single layer if you have split breast pieces) and sprinkle with the salt. Add the bay leaves, garlic, carrot, peppercorns, and coriander seeds, if using, along with enough cold water to cover the chicken by about 1 inch.

2 Set the pot over medium-low heat and cook until bubbles begin to form around the edges. Once they do, reduce the heat to low to make sure that the cooking water maintains a temperature between 170 and 180°F (77–82°C). Cook until the chicken is cooked all the way through, 15 to 18 minutes; an instant-read thermometer should register 160°F (70°C) at the thickest part of the breast. If it's not cooked through, cook it longer, checking it every 1 to 2 minutes.

3 Turn the heat off and immediately remove the chicken from the pot, reserving the poaching liquid. Allow the meat to rest and, once cool enough to handle, remove the skin and pull the meat from the bone, shredding or cutting it as desired. If not using immediately, pack the meat in a sealed container with enough poaching liquid to cover it to help keep it moist, and store in the refrigerator for up to 5 days.

Leftover Chicken Pot Pie

4–6 servings

INGREDIENTS

- 3 tablespoons unsalted butter, plus more for greasing the casserole dish
- 3 carrots, thinly sliced into coins
- 3 stalks celery, thinly sliced
- 1 leek, cleaned and chopped
- 1 tablespoon fresh thyme
- ½ teaspoon salt
- ½ teaspoon freshly ground black pepper
- 2 cups chopped or pulled chicken
- 5 ounces mushrooms, such as shiitake or chanterelle, wiped clean and chopped
- ½ cup white wine or chicken stock (page 99)
- 2 cups milk (or a combination of milk and heavy cream)
- ¼ cup all-purpose flour
- Zest of ½ a lemon
- 2 sheets (14 to 16 ounces) puff pastry, thawed
- 1 egg, lightly beaten

This recipe started as a Thanksgiving tradition, until one day it dawned on me that it's also the perfect way to use leftover roast or poached chicken. Eventually I realized that it's the perfect way to use *any* leftover chicken.

I admit that it takes a bit more work than throwing leftovers in between two tortillas with preshredded cheese, but the extra effort also stretches two cups of meat into a rich, hearty dinner that can feed up to six people!

1 Preheat the oven to 400°F (200°C) and butter a 2-quart casserole dish; set aside. Melt 2 tablespoons of the butter in a large sauté pan set over medium heat. Add the carrots, celery, leek, thyme, salt, and pepper. Sauté until the vegetables are just tender, 8 to 10 minutes.

2 Add the chicken, along with any accumulated juices or gelatin, and the mushrooms, stirring well to combine, and cook for 2 minutes. Add the wine and cook until all of the runny liquid has evaporated, being mindful not to dry out the chicken. Transfer the chicken and vegetables to a large mixing bowl.

3 Wipe the pan clean and return it to medium heat. Melt the remaining 1 tablespoon butter. Add 1 cup of the milk and, with a whisk ready in hand, sprinkle the flour over it. Whisk until no lumps remain, then add the remaining 1 cup milk. Cook until the sauce thickens, about 3 minutes, whisking periodically for the first couple of minutes and constantly for the last 30 seconds or so, before removing the pan from the heat.

4 Add the white sauce and the lemon zest to the mixing bowl with the chicken and vegetables; toss to combine well. Taste, then adjust the zest, salt, and pepper as desired. Pour the chicken and vegetable filling into the prepped casserole dish and top with both sheets of puff pastry, overlapping them by an inch and gently pressing to seal them together to prevent leaking. Using a paring knife, cut a few slits into the top of the puff pastry crust and brush with the egg. Place in the oven and bake, uncovered, for 25 to 30 minutes, until the dough puffs and turns golden brown. Allow to cool for 5 to 10 minutes before serving.

My Ultimate Chicken Salad

2 servings

INGREDIENTS

- 1 cup chopped or shredded chicken (see Poached Chicken, pages 144–45)
- 2 tablespoons chopped chives or scallions, green parts only
- ½ cup chopped grapes
- ¼ cup toasted slivered almonds
- 3 tablespoons mayonnaise
- 2 tablespoons chopped fresh dill
- 2 teaspoons Dijon mustard
- 2 teaspoons sour cream
- Salt
- Freshly ground black pepper

I used to call this Fancy Pants Chicken Salad because it's the kind of chicken salad you can serve on croissants. Though truth be told, it works just as well on sliced white, too, which is why I renamed the recipe.

You can make a few substitutions to this recipe in a pinch. You can use celery instead of grapes for that refreshing crunch. You can substitute pecans for almonds. Either way, if you buy nuts preroasted and salted, be sure to taste the salad with the nuts added before you season it with salt.

One last note: I wrote the recipe based on just 1 cup of leftover chicken, but if you want to make this salad for a crowd, adjust the recipe up without worrying too much about exact amounts. It's not *that* fancy.

Add the chicken, chives, grapes, almonds, mayonnaise, dill, mustard, and sour cream to a medium mixing bowl. Using a wooden spoon or silicon spatula, gently fold until well combined. Season with salt and pepper as desired. Serve on your bread of choice — or eat straight out of the bowl.

Party–Size Chili Queso Dip

Makes 2 quarts

INGREDIENTS

- 4 tablespoons unsalted butter, plus more for greasing the casserole dish
- 2 tablespoons neutral oil, such as grapeseed
- 1 (4-ounce) can green chiles, preferably fire-roasted
- 2 scallions, trimmed and chopped, white and green parts
- ½ red bell pepper, finely chopped
- 1 (15-ounce) can cannellini beans, drained and rinsed
- 1 cup leftover chopped or shredded chicken, or however much you have on hand (see Poached Chicken, pages 144–45)
- 3 tablespoons all-purpose flour
- ½ teaspoon garlic powder
- ¼ teaspoon ground cumin
- ¼ teaspoon paprika
- 1 cup milk (whole milk preferable, but any kind will work)
- 3 cups (12 ounces) shredded pepper Jack cheese
- ¼ cup sour cream
- Fresh cilantro (optional)
- Tortillas chips, for serving

You know how in the days after Halloween there's always an onslaught of articles about how to use up leftover Halloween candy? It's funny to me how half of them suggest baking candy in cookies and brownies, and the other half suggest adding candy to candy (looking at you, Halloween bark). It's like: *Hey, get rid of that candy by doubling down on the sugar!*

You know what? I like it! It's gutsy and fun, and we only live once. This recipe is kind of like the chicken version of that.

It takes leftovers — and I'm going to assume that you made something fabulously delicious in the first place — and doubles down on them by adding butter and cheese and milk and sour cream. Oh my! Be sure to invite all your friends over to enjoy this with you. It's that good, plus two quarts is really a lot of dip.

1. Preheat the oven to 375°F (190°C) and lightly butter a 2-quart casserole dish; set aside. In the meantime, heat the oil in a medium pot set over medium heat and sauté the chiles, scallions, and bell pepper until all of the liquid cooks off, about 5 minutes. Transfer the vegetables to a large bowl and combine with the beans and chicken; set aside.

2. Wipe down the pot and return it to the stove over medium heat. Melt the butter; as soon as it begins to foam, add the flour, garlic powder, cumin, and paprika. Cook, whisking constantly, until the entire surface foams, 1 to 2 minutes. Turn the heat off and add the milk in a slow steady stream, continuing to whisk constantly.

   As soon as the mixture is smooth, turn the heat back to medium and add 1½ cups — about half — of the cheese in three separate additions, whisking each addition smooth before adding the next. Once you whisk in the last bit of cheese, turn the heat off and whisk in the sour cream, too.

3. Pour the cheese sauce over the chicken and other ingredients in the bowl, and using a wooden spoon or silicone spatula, fold to combine well. Transfer the mixture to the prepped casserole dish and top with the remaining 1½ cups cheese.

   Bake for about 20 minutes, then turn the broiler to high and transfer to the broiler for 3 to 5 minutes to brown the cheese on top. Allow the dip to rest for at least 5 minutes before topping with cilantro, if using, and serving with tons of your favorite tortilla chips.

Ten-Minute Tostad

4 servings

INGREDIENTS

8–12 store-bought tosta-
das (2 or 3 tostadas
per person)

Favorite store-
bought bean dip

4 cups leftover
chopped or shred-
ded chicken, or
however much you
have on hand (see
Poached Chicken,
pages 144–45)

1½ cups (6 ounces)
shredded cheddar
or Monterey Jack
cheese

Favorite tostada
garnishes, such as
shredded lettuce,
avocado, pico de
gallo, sour cream,
pickled or thinly
sliced fresh jala-
peños, and cilantro

This is hardly a recipe, but it's my current favorite example of how
leftover chicken — or, even better, prepped-ahead Poached Chicke
(pages 144–45) — is an absolute lifesaver.

With chicken already cooked and waiting, and the rest of the
regularly stocked in my pantry and fridge, I know that there's *alwa*
well-balanced dinner that I can pull together in ten minutes.

1 Lay the tostadas on a sheet pan.
Dollop some bean dip on each
one and, using the back of a
spoon, spread the dip into a thin
layer covering each tostada.

2 Place the chicken on top of the
bean dip, being careful not to
pile it too high or it won't heat
through; if using poached chicken,
spoon a little bit of the poaching
liquid from the storage container
over the meat to help keep it
moist while it reheats. Top with
the shredded cheese, dividing it
equally among the tostadas.

3 Heat the broiler to
the sheet pan under
5 minutes, until the
and the edges of th
turn a deep golden
carefully, as the tos
quickly.

4 Remove the tostad
oven and top with y
garnishes. Serve im

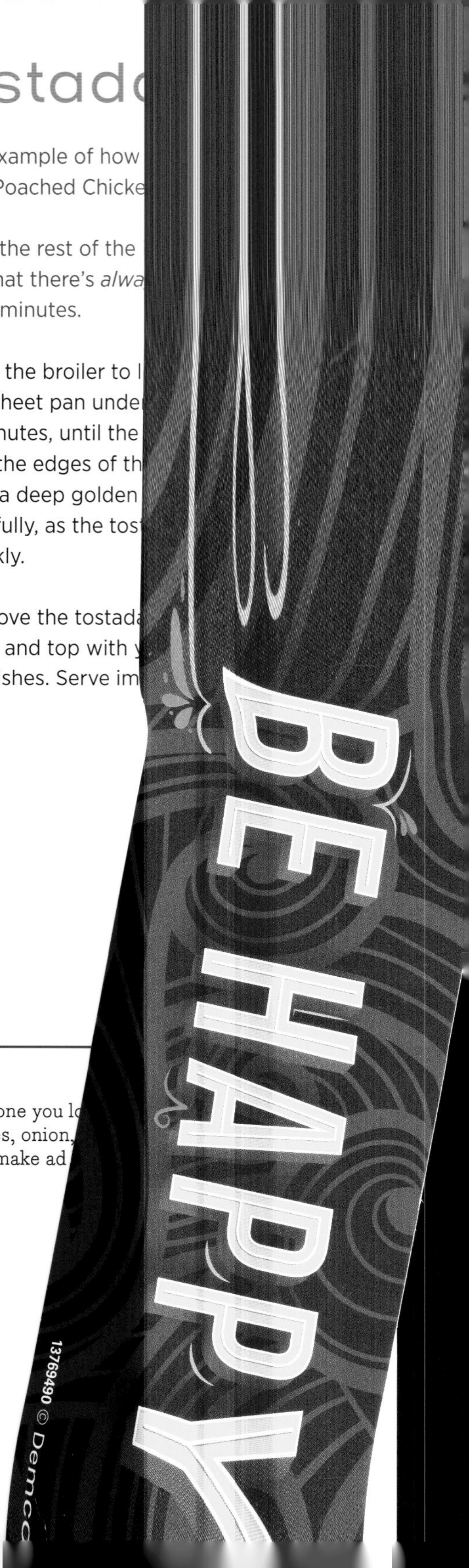

COOK'S NOTES

Look for tostadas that are made without preservatives.

I'm not a huge fan of most jarred salsas, though if there's one you lo
grab fresh pico de gallo or just chop some cherry tomatoes, onion,
them into 1 or 2 ripe avocados with lime juice and salt to make a d

BE HAPPY

13769490 © Demco

METRIC CONVERSIONS

Unless you have finely calibrated measuring equipment, conversions between U.S. and metric measurements will be somewhat inexact. It's important to convert the measurements for all of the ingredients in a recipe to maintain the same proportions as the original.

WEIGHT

To convert	to	multiply
ounces	grams	ounces by 28.35
pounds	grams	pounds by 453.5
pounds	kilograms	pounds by 0.45

US	Metric
0.035 ounce	1 gram
¼ ounce	7 grams
½ ounce	14 grams
1 ounce	28 grams
1¼ ounces	35 grams
1½ ounces	40 grams
1¾ ounces	50 grams
2½ ounces	70 grams
3½ ounces	100 grams
4 ounces	112 grams
5 ounces	140 grams
8 ounces	228 grams
8¾ ounces	250 grams
10 ounces	280 grams
15 ounces	425 grams
16 ounces (1 pound)	454 grams

VOLUME

To convert	to	multiply
teaspoons	milliliters	teaspoons by 4.93
tablespoons	milliliters	tablespoons by 14.79
fluid ounces	milliliters	fluid ounces by 29.57
cups	milliliters	cups by 236.59
cups	liters	cups by 0.24
pints	milliliters	pints by 473.18
pints	liters	pints by 0.473
quarts	milliliters	quarts by 946.36
quarts	liters	quarts by 0.946
gallons	liters	gallons by 3.785

US	Metric
1 teaspoon	5 milliliters
1 tablespoon	15 milliliters
¼ cup	60 milliliters
½ cup	120 milliliters
1 cup	240 milliliters
1¼ cups	300 milliliters
1½ cups	355 milliliters
2 cups	480 milliliters
2½ cups	600 milliliters
3 cups	710 milliliters
4 cups (1 quart)	0.95 liter
4 quarts (1 gallon)	3.8 liters

RECITE LIST

IN AN OVEN

IN A PAN

IN A POT

ON A GRILL

USING AND CREATING LEFTOVERS

DRESSINGS/MARINADES/SAUCES

INDEX

Numbers in *italic* indicate photos.

SOLVE DINNERTIME DILEMMAS
WITH MORE BOOKS FROM STOREY

Build-a-Bowl by Nicki Sizemore

With this fuss-free formula, you can create 77 delicious and nourishing grain bowls for any meal of the day, from Sunshine Citrus and Coconut Cream to Curry-Roasted Salmon and Pork Banh Mi Bowls. Countless customizing options help you suit individual diets and tastes.

Cast-Iron Cooking by Rachael Narins

Make your skillet sizzle! These 40 recipes show off the versatility of this affordable and timeless cooking method, from cast-iron classics like cornbread, pan pizza, and the perfect grilled cheese sandwich to future favorites like Korean fried chicken, skillet catfish, and s'mores.

Fresh Flavors for the Slow Cooker by Nicki Sizemore

Revamp your slow cooker repertoire with 77 recipes that emphasize fresh ingredients, flavorful herbs and spices, and ease of preparation. Do-ahead tips and recipes for sides, salads, and sauces turn delicious dishes, from carnitas tacos to veggie lasagna, into well-rounded meals.

The Make-Ahead Sauce Solution by Elisabeth Bailey

Transform your weeknight dinners with these 62 make-ahead, freezer-friendly sauces. Flavor-packed classics like All-American Barbecue and Sausage Ragu join creative combinations such as Chorizo Garlic, Pumpkin Coconut Cream, and Gorgonzola-Chive Butter, ensuring there's something for every taste.

JOIN THE CONVERSATION. Share your experience with this book, learn more about Storey Publishing's authors, and read original essays and book excerpts at storey.com. Look for our books wherever quality books are sold or call 800-441-5700.